Excerpt from the Foreword

However, as they pulled up to the door of our home, I experienced a sensation that literally sent love energy up and down my spine. The man whose work I had studied some 15 years earlier, who had written the classic book on higher consciousness, was being lifted from the car to a wheelchair by his wife, Penny. I simply had no idea that Ken had spent the previous 40 years—yes, I said 40 years of his life—in a wheelchair paralyzed by polio throughout most of his body. This man was in my living room [in 1985] with the most peaceful and loving demeanor of anyone I had ever encountered—a living example of all that he had talked about in his wonderful books.

That feeling of love that I felt as Ken sat in his wheelchair with us that evening came from the inner realization that this was an example of a truly remarkable being. He had two choices after becoming crippled as a young man: 1) feel sorry for himself and ask, "Why me?" or 2) go beyond his form, and teach others about their own personal transformational possibilities without even mentioning that his own form was restricted to a wheelchair and a lifetime as a quadriplegic. Is it any wonder that I have so much admiration for this man? He not only writes about transformation and higher consciousness, it was his destiny to live it each and every day, and ultimately to become a role model for all of us.

Author

Discovering the Secrets of Happiness:
My Intimate Story

Discovering the Secrets of Happiness:
My Intimate Story

Ken Keyes, Jr.

First Printing

LOVE LINE BOOKS
Coos Bay, Oregon 97420

Your purchase of any Love Line book helps to build a more loving and caring world. The author receives no royalties. All surplus goes to a nonprofit organization dedicated to teaching Living Love and the Science of Happiness.

Discovering the Secrets of Happiness may be obtained through your local bookstore, or you may order it from the Ken Keyes College Bookroom, 790 Commercial Avenue, Coos Bay, OR 97420 for $7.95 plus $1.50 for postage and handling.

Up to five pages of this book may be freely quoted or reprinted without permission, provided credit is given in the following form:

Reprinted from *Discovering the Secrets of Happiness: My Intimate Story* by Ken Keyes, Jr. Copyright 1989 by Love Line Books.

First Printing: 1989 50,000 copies

Library of Congress Cataloging-in-Publication Data

Keyes, Ken.
    Discovering the secrets of happiness.
    1 Happiness. 2. Self-actualization (Psychology)
3. Self-actualization (Psychology)--Case studies.
4. Keyes, Ken. 5. Psychologists--Oregon--Biography.
I. Title.
BF575.H27K48 1989   158'.1'0924 [B]   88-8316
ISBN 0-915972-15-8

LOVE LINE BOOKS
700 Commercial Avenue, Coos Bay, OR 97420

To those who build
the future of humanity
by opening
their hearts with
understanding, patience,
and generosity for
their fellow humans.

Contents

IV Finding the Love in My Heart

Acknowledgments

I am deeply appreciative of the help from Liz Moore, Jean Rukkila, Bill Starkey, Jim Twyman, and Aura Wright, who read the manuscript and gave me many helpful suggestions.

Ann Hauser cheerfully and patiently typeset the manuscript with its countless changes, and made valuable recommendations for improving the content. My wife, Penny, has played the roles of editor and proofreader, and constantly aided and encouraged me.

Dave Carrothers helped me present the personal growth story of my life in a clearer and more interesting way. Bill Hannig offered various design ideas that have added to the attractiveness of the format. Marjorie Tully assisted in the proofreading. Catrina Moss helped me in the polishing process. Dave Wegferd used unusual diligence to make excellent halftone negatives of the photos.

To these and many others, I give my heartfelt appreciation.

Foreword

Dr. Wayne Dyer
Author, *Your Erroneous Zones*

My first reaction to receiving this wonderful new manuscript from Ken was, "It's about time." It is time for the entire world to know about the human being in back of all those empowering books produced by Ken Keyes. Most of the people that I encounter are well aware of his magnificent publications. Yet very few know about Ken himself. And it is in getting to know this amazing human being that his writings will become all the more meaningful and influential. I am thrilled to be writing the foreword to Ken's own personal story. And before you even begin to devour this exciting book, I would like to introduce you to the man I have known and loved personally.

It seems like centuries ago, and yet it was only back in the early seventies, that I first picked up the *Handbook to Higher Consciousness* written by an unknown, to me, author named Ken Keyes, Jr. This powerful book was to have a profound effect on my own consciousness, for it propelled me into an entirely new way of thinking and acting in my own personal and professional life. I was deeply touched by the exquisite messages offered up in the *Handbook*, and I literally carried it with me wherever

I traveled throughout the seventies. I kept a copy in my automobile, another in my bedroom on the night table, and a third in the bathroom, where I would review the contents of this or that page on a daily basis. I knew Ken's words, yet I still knew nothing of the man. I was deeply touched by the concepts he wrote about, and in many ways they provided me with my earliest motivation to pursue higher consciousness in my own books, tapes, and films.

In the early 1980's I was again introduced to an entirely new way of thinking and being when a copy of *The Hundredth Monkey* arrived at my office. I was moved by the sincerity in which this beautifully simple book was written. I began to know within that a collective consciousness was much more than the dreamy meanderings of a few metaphysical types. This book led me to investigate and write about the idea that thoughts were much more powerful than most people had ever considered.

I learned more about the notions of critical mass, collective consciousness, and synchronicity as useful tools for making a big difference in the world. I had been introduced to all of this exciting new literature by the man I am introducing here in this book. Once again, Ken Keyes, Jr. had played a large role in turning my life around.

I began to nurture like seedlings such ideas as: The power of love is enormous. We can create thought. We are all connected by thought. Out of thought comes the entire direction of our lives. We act on our thoughts. We literally become what we think about all day long, both as individuals and as a people. In the dimensionless world of thought, everything we think is already here. We have the ability to turn any thought into form with the power of mind. Thought is a formless energy which comprises our essential humanity. Our lives are what our thoughts create.

These ideas could literally transform our entire species and turn our divisiveness and separateness as a human family into one of cooperation and harmony forever. Ken Keyes literally got me started on this glorious transformational journey.

In 1983 I wrote my own parable about a higher human being named Eykis who visits our world with the messages of enlightenment and higher consciousness. When it was published, I sent a copy off to Ken at his college in Coos Bay, Oregon, never expecting to hear any more. It was simply a gift from one person on the path to a very special pathfinder who had played such a large, joyful role in my own growth as a human being. To my surprise, I received a reply and a note indicating that he would be in South Florida in a few months, and that he would love to spend an evening together.

I was delighted and, sure enough, it all came about. Ken and Penny arrived at our home to spend an enchanting evening together with our young children. Later at a favorite restaurant of ours, my wife, Marcie, and I, along with Penny and Ken, feasted on a sumptuous meal of original Thai food.

However, as they pulled up to the door of our home, I experienced a sensation that literally sent love energy up and down my spine. The man whose work I had studied some 15 years earlier, who had written the classic book on higher consciousness, was being lifted from the car to a wheelchair by his wife, Penny. I simply had no idea that Ken had spent the previous 40 years— yes, I said 40 years of his life—in a wheelchair paralyzed by polio throughout most of his body. This man was in my living room with the most peaceful and loving demeanor of anyone I had ever encountered—a living example of all that he had talked about in his wonderful books.

I know today that there are no accidents in this perfect universe, and that everything happens precisely the way it is supposed to happen. One never truly awakens until they are able to go beyond the boundaries of the body, and it was Ken's experience of being rendered paralyzed at the age of 25 that provided him with the "opportunity" to literally go beyond the boundaries of his form. It hit me as I saw this beautiful human being that he had written the *Handbook to Higher Consciousness,* explaining to all of us how to become transformed, and he was a living, breathing example of having done just that himself.

Look at the word "form" and ponder what it means. Your body is form. The packaging that houses your true humanity is all form. Yet your essential humanity is in the dimensionless formless world of thoughts. Now place the prefix "trans" (which means to go beyond) in front of "form," and the suffix "tion" (which means the result or experience of) after the word "form"—and you have a new word, "transformation," the result or experience of going beyond your form.

It seems to me that Ken Keyes's destiny, if you will, was to live in that place where he had to soar beyond his form because his form simply was not functioning. Yet he still was able to not only live a transcendent life, but to help millions of others do the same thing—and never once even tell anyone that he was a consciousness trapped in a form that he had to soar above.

That feeling of love that I felt as Ken sat in his wheelchair with us that evening came from the inner realization that this was an example of a truly remarkable being. He had two choices after becoming crippled as a young man: 1) feel sorry for himself and ask, "Why me?" or 2) go beyond his form, and teach others about their own personal transformational possibilities without even mentioning that his own form was restricted to a wheelchair and a lifetime as a quadriplegic. Is it any wonder that I have so much admiration for this man? He not only writes about transformation and higher consciousness, it was his destiny to live it each and every day, and ultimately to become a role model for all of us.

I am honored to have been asked to write the foreword to Ken's personal story. I encouraged him to write it, and I am proud to introduce this transcendent human being to you, the reader, who will relive his blatantly honest account of his own journey.

In my own heart, I know that we are not human beings having a spiritual experience, but rather spiritual beings having a human experience. Ken Keyes, Jr. is one example of a person who has coalesced the human and the spiritual into one being, who is a living example of "trans-form-ation" in action. I am confident that you will discover this for yourself in this transcendent account of Ken's own personal experience.

In love and light,
Wayne Dyer

Part I
The Search for Happiness

1

My Life Is a Surprise

"I have a surprise for you," Penny told me as we were having dinner at a Chinese restaurant one evening. Penny is my wonderful co-adventurer in the great game of life (also known as my helpmate, lover, and wife).

"Is it a gift?" I asked.

"Yes, in a way," she replied.

"Can you buy it in a store?"

"Not now."

"Could it fit in a small box?"

"Yes."

"Do I have one already?"

"No," she answered.

Usually I can narrow the possibilities and nail it down. I was getting nowhere.

The next morning she walked into my office with Dave, who was then the administrator of our personal growth college. He had suggested the surprise. I looked them over—wondering if they were hiding the package. Penny's eyes sparkled as Dave cleared his throat.

"Ken, it's time you wrote your story for everyone to read," he said.

"I'll help any way I can," Penny added.

I must have looked puzzled. No wonder I couldn't guess. I was expecting a tangible gift. She was right; this was a real surprise.

I had to admit I'd had fleeting thoughts that perhaps someday, when I was too senile to do anything else, I might tell the story of my life—but right now I was too busy. We were just about to print a grassroots book on how we, the people, can create peace and prosperity in this nuclear age, and I was helping the staff of our college get through its adolescent growing pains. It had been three and a half years since Penny and I had taken a vacation. The last one was our month-long honeymoon on Aruba, an island off the coast of South America. I needed something else to do? This was indeed a surprise.

Accepting the Gift

I quickly decided that I couldn't turn down such a "gift." I wasn't interested in writing a step-by-step account of my life from infancy to adulthood through marriage, and so forth. What I really wanted was to openly share my own experience, and how I'd learned to successfully meet my life's toughest challenges.

I had found how to sustain a level of happiness and love that I considered most unusual, and I wanted to share these beautiful "secrets" with the world. I decided it was time to "go public" with my intimate story.

In my zigzags up the ladder of happiness, I have discovered some powerful breakthrough methods that helped me grow at an extraordinary rate. These new techniques have helped me free myself from unfortunate mental habits that I, like most people, picked up in early childhood. Many "awful" things have happened to me. I've learned how to take the catastrophes, problems, and frustrations that life has thrown at me and use them for my personal growth. Although they didn't seem that way at the time, I now regard them as "gifts" from the universe. It's like turning a sour lemon into lemonade.

I think the real story of my life is more inside than outside. What is it that has triggered my feelings of security, insecurity, worry, anger, joy, love, happiness, or unhappiness? What are the lessons life has offered me through sex, relationships, money, marriages, possessions, prestige, pride, success, appreciation, and love for myself and others—or the lack of these? How do I deal with the mental habits (I like to call them programmings) that have generated my unpleasant feelings and experiences?

As I've grown, I have less and less use for personal privacy. I tell myself there's nothing in my life today—even in my innermost thoughts—that I think I need to hide from anyone. (When I want to hide something from you, I make you an *other*—not one of *us*. I don't keep secrets from *us*; I only try to hide things from people I consider as *them*.) I feel I'm breathing fully and freely when I live in honesty and openness with everybody about everything in my life.

I invite you to come inside my life and feelings; to examine my habits of thinking, my thoughts, and my illusions; and to follow my ups and downs, my "failures" and "successes"—so you may experience the adventures that have enabled me to discover the secrets of happiness.

Twee's Gift of Self-Esteem

My father, Kenneth Scofield Keyes, was born and reared in Michigan; my mother, Lucille Marcia Thomas, was a Southern belle living in Atlanta. They met while my father was in officers' training school in Chattanooga during World War I. The war ended in November 1918 before he was sent overseas to France. After marrying my mother, he set up a partnership in an advertising agency in Atlanta.

I first opened my eyes at 1:45 a.m. on January 19, 1921. I called my mother "Twee." I'm told I tried to say "sweetie" and it came out "Tweetie"—afterward shortened to "Twee." She later told me that her mother often severely berated her and made her feel inadequate as she was growing up. Because of this, Twee developed feelings of insecurity and inferiority. Although she was very talented (author, poet, coloratura soprano), she eventually began overusing alcohol as a way to relax the grip of her feelings of insecurity.

Twee wanted me to grow up with the self-confidence she never had. As I look back now, I can see how she did everything she could to bolster my self-esteem. I recall lying in bed (perhaps around age six) while she gently stroked me as I fell asleep. She would tell me, "When you grow up, you will be able to achieve anything you want." Objectively I know this is non-sense. I can't do *anything* I want. But *inside* I usually *feel* that I can if I'm willing to put in enough effort. I've had no hesitation in carefully planning a number of bold things, unfettered by self-doubts. Some have worked;

some haven't. I've learned from the ones that didn't. The ones that worked have given me a lot of satisfaction. No way to lose—either way I've gained something valuable.

Twee also told me when I was a child, "When you grow up, if you and I ever disagree about anything, you follow your own thoughts." Wow! She must have felt quite hurt and smothered as a child. She evidently made a far-reaching decision to nurture the self-confidence of her young son. I don't remember her ever telling me things such as "You're a bad boy" or "You'll never learn to do things right." She was a fiery redhead who could get quite upset with me at times—but she never seemed to slash *at me*. It was always at what I'd done.

I feel that by her nurturing my self-confidence and self-esteem, she helped me avoid many of the ravages of insecurity and self-doubt that are often imprinted during the first few years of life. I always felt she would love and support me unconditionally even though she might not understand or approve of what I was doing. This, to me, is one of the most precious gifts a parent can give a child. Twee and my dog, Schnapps, were my main models of unconditional love in my life.

Moving to Miami

I was often sick with chronic bronchitis and croup. The doctor told my parents that I would have better health in the sunny climate of southern Florida. So we moved to Miami Beach in 1925. South Florida was having a huge land boom in which one could buy a vacant lot and perhaps sell it for double the next month. Eventually the boom exploded, and prices drastically plummeted from where they had been driven by speculative fever. Most of the investors (who knew

My mother
and father

In my boyhood

nothing of writing leases, collecting rents, and fixing leaky roofs) were unable to sell their properties after the bubble burst. My father seized the opportunity to set up a business managing these income properties.

He usually went to the office before 7 a.m. and worked evenings at home. From the very beginning he built his business on sincerity and honesty. "Give to the world the best that you have, and the best will come back to you" was (and still is) printed on his office memos. As his reputation grew, he built up a large management business. The speculators eventually sold their investments. The Keyes Company developed over the next few decades into the largest real estate firm in the southern states. I know I benefited by his example of self-confidence and willingness to work hard to achieve his goals.

My father became active in the evangelical wing of the Presbyterian Church. Over the years he became a deacon and elder. He wrote a pamphlet on tithing, and millions of copies have been distributed. He has often been invited to give Sunday sermons at churches throughout the United States.

Unless I was sick, he always took me to Sunday school. When I was eight years old, I began to examine critically some of the things I was being taught in Sunday school. I did not talk to my father about these concerns, for I felt that he would disapprove of my doubts. Nevertheless, I continued going to church with him through my high school years.

My great-grandfather, a wealthy Atlanta businessman, had built a baronial family estate in the mountains near Clayton, Georgia. It was called Kingwood. Until I was 12, Twee always took me to Kingwood to be with her family during the three hot summer months. The white two-story mansion had a 100-foot-long front porch with large columns. Papa King's many daughters each had her own bedroom. There were other rooms for the older grandchildren. I loved playing with my cousins and being with so many relatives. I remember poking around the barn, picking apples off the trees, and splitting watermelons on the vine with my cousin King Hart. Thinking about those times brings up warm feelings and pleasant memories.

My father's business kept expanding, and we moved to a nicer home every two or three years. We usually lived in a neighborhood where there were few playmates my age. As an only (and sometimes lonely) child, I grew up in the prosperous community of Greater Miami and climbed the educational ladder from the Coral Gables Elementary School through Miami High School.

Throughout my boyhood, I had many hobbies: stamp collecting, playing the Hawaiian guitar, and model railroading. I raised parakeets—I called them "love birds." I would split coconuts that fell from the trees around our house, take out the big nuts and some of the fibrous material, and put them back together. In each one I'd cut a small opening at one end just big enough for a bird to squeeze through, hang it from the top of the birdhouse, and soon there would be eggs and then baby birds. I sold the green birds for a dollar, and the rarer blue and white ones went for as much as five to ten dollars back in the 1930's.

I also enjoyed woodworking and had a workshop with a power-driven circular saw, jigsaw, planer, and sander. I made a custom magazine rack that I sold to a drugstore, a breadboard for our kitchen, and a tile top mahogany table for our living room.

For three summers while I was in junior high, my parents sent me to Camp Dixie for Boys. The eight weeks of summer camp offered me many challenges: I was not very good at helping my cabin win games through baseball, tennis, and other athletic competitions. I was not popular. And I had the problem of hiding the fact that I sometimes wet my bed. In spite of all that, I looked forward to going to camp. The full schedule of games, swimming, crafts, horseback trips, and hikes—and the playmates—attracted me.

When I was in high school, we moved to a house overlooking Biscayne Bay in Miami. My father bought me a 16-foot Bahama-built sailboat for $75. It had a jib, a mainsail, and a small cabin. Thus began my lifelong love affair with the water.

My Experiment With Belle

I enjoyed going to school, and this showed in my grades. All A's were the rule, B's a tragedy, and C's almost nonexistent. In the ninth grade at Shenandoah Junior High School, I was assigned to Belle Hancock's English class. Belle was a homely, middle-aged teacher known for unusual strictness. The qualities of kindness, compassion, and understanding were rarely attributed to her by her students. On the first day of class, students rushed to sit in the back seats of her room; the front row was entirely vacant.

Somehow the contrarian in me (or was it the achiever?) decided to take a chance. I not only sat in the front row but I chose the chair next to her desk. I made it a point

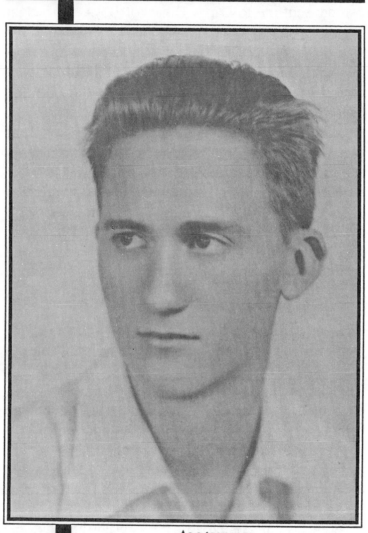

As a teenager

to speak with her as often as I could. Belle was good at explaining English grammar with its nominative and objective cases, and particularly the structural diagramming of sentences. Although I was not really interested in grammar, I tried to pay attention to her teaching.

Popular rumor had it that she gave A students B's, B students C's, and failed all C students. In my first semester in her class, my tests and homework averaged 89.5. One had to average 90 or more to get an A. I knew the best I could hope for was a semester grade of B. When I received my report card, I was astounded to find that she had given me an A. Belle even showed me her records of my grades. My average merited only a high B!

I never ratted on her; her reputation for strictness was secure with me. I was beginning to learn that when I express caring and friendliness, they are reflected back to me in life. This was a valuable lesson, and it even works with the Belle Hancocks of the world. Perhaps it works especially with the Belle Hancocks. It's easy to quickly generalize about a particular person and treat him or her accordingly. My experience with Belle planted the seed of a system of behavior based on caring, cooperation, and friendliness. But the seed took a long time to sprout.

Learning on My Own

In 1938 I entered Duke University in Durham, North Carolina so I could share college life with my best friend, Graham Miller. In my sophomore year, I concluded that I could educate myself several times faster than in the usual college classroom system. I wanted to read up to eight hours a day in self-initiated study—not for grades or credentials but for knowledge.

At my parents' summer home on Lake Santeetlah in western North Carolina, I met Dr. William McCall of Teachers College, Columbia University—a scholar and friend who was to have a profound influence in my life. He was well-known for his work on measurement in education. He had devised the McCall Intelligence Test, authored the "Standard Test Lessons in Reading" (widely used in elementary schools throughout the nation), and invented the T-Score (a statistical measure of deviation from the norm). McCall had contracted tuberculosis, the disease had been arrested, and he was living in semi-retirement at his home on the lake.

Will McCall and I realized immediately that we shared common interests. I told him of my desire to run my own study course without going to classes. He explained to me that this was the system used in some European universities. Based on his encouragement, my father agreed to support me for two years in self-guided study beginning in the spring of 1940. I also enrolled in several music courses at the University of Miami. I studied voice with Arturo di Fillippi.

During a lesson one day, di Fillippi and I got to talking about staging an opera—and decided to do it. In the music stores throughout Miami I put out notices announcing the opera, and singers who were interested met in my parents' home. We began rehearsals for *Pagliacci*, and di Fillippi sang the leading tenor part. Our production was so successful that we established the Miami Opera Guild, which has continued to this day.

In 1941 the clouds of war were gathering rapidly over the United States. Instead of waiting to be drafted, I enlisted in a naval unit set up that summer in Miami to censor cablegrams going in and out of the United States if war began. The cable censorship office could stop, alter, or delay suspicious cablegrams in which Nazi agents might hide military intelligence. Since I preferred an office job in Miami to combat overseas, I welcomed this way to serve my country. Everyone assigned to this intelligence office lived at home during their service.

My First Marriage

When I was 20, I met Roberta Rymer at the University of Miami. She played the piano accompaniment at my lessons with di Fillippi. She had a dramatic soprano voice and also studied with di Fillippi. After about a year, we had our first date. We enjoyed each other's company so much that we found ourselves wanting the togetherness of marriage. We became engaged in the fall and planned a wedding on December 12, 1941. Meanwhile, without first consulting us, the Japanese made a surprise attack on Pearl Harbor in Hawaii on December 7th. War was declared. All military leaves were canceled. The honeymoon we'd planned became a weekend at the Sovereign Hotel on Miami Beach.

Although I had met several of Roberta's relatives before we were married, she never mentioned that her father had founded one of the nation's largest stove factories. I only became aware of this after we were married when substantial dividend checks started coming. It was a pleasant surprise, since the Navy only paid me around $144 per month plus housing and dependent's allowance.

During the war I worked aboard what was affectionately called the "U.S.S. DuPont," a large new office building in downtown Miami. I was eventually promoted to chief petty officer in a naval intelligence photo lab. My son, Ken III, was born on December 6, 1942 and my daughter, Clara Lu, arrived on April 4, 1944. Because of my service for over four years, I was one of the first to be discharged from the Navy after the war ended. In October 1945, I began working with my father in his real estate business.

Back in the forties black people could not associate with whites at lunch counters, hotels, and schools, and they were forced to sit in the back of buses. We wondered what part we could play to help change these attitudes. We bought 45 acres south of Miami, hoping to set up and run a demonstration project in which five orphans from each race of humankind could grow up in loving harmony together. But I got wrapped up in business and it never happened.

Roberta and I enjoyed our young lives with Kenny and Clara Lu. We felt we had all we needed. We were a cozy family of four with a beautiful home. Basically, life was peaceful.

And then in February 1946, I was hit in an out-of-season polio epidemic. Both of my legs and the fingers of my left hand became totally paralyzed and the fingers of my right hand generally so. Functioning arm muscles were few, although some back and abdominal muscles survived. In one week I had gone from a 25-year-old businessman to a convalescent who needed constant assistance just to stay alive. By medical definition, I was left 100 percent disabled. Life had thrown me a lemon. How do you make lemonade from that? How could I deal with this calamity—*or was it really a calamity?*

2

Making the Wheelchair Disappear

At first the polio attack felt like a bad case of flu in which I ached all over. Pretty soon the aching was far more intense than any flu, and my spinal column felt like it was on fire. I was taken to Jackson Memorial Hospital, and a spinal tap confirmed I had polio. I had been able to walk into the hospital; within a few days paralysis developed in my legs, hands, arms, and many body muscles. Treatment consisted mainly of wrapping my arms and legs in hot, itchy, moist wool blankets to relax the contracted muscles.

During the first month I was in constant pain and could hardly wait to get my nightly shot of Demerol that would let me get to sleep. At my request Roberta brought over my sound equipment and classical albums for me to listen to. After several weeks, they lifted me into a wheelchair. I could endure sitting in it for five minutes—and then it was back to bed. From then on, each day I was able to sit up in a wheelchair for a little longer time.

My last photo taken before polio
with Roberta by the plane that flew me
to Warm Springs several months later

(It took about three months to be able to sit up as long as I wanted without rear end pain.)

After about a month I talked my doctor into letting me take an ambulance ride around the city, lying flat the whole time. It was one of the most enjoyable experiences I have ever had. Somehow the old familiar streets and buildings seemed to go into a new dimension. Sights that I had previously taken for granted as I routinely drove about the city now looked fresh, new, and delightful. I was struck by the relative nature of happiness. It seemed to depend not on what was happening but on how I received and responded to what was happening.

My parents were advised that the best place for me to convalesce from polio was the Warm Springs Foundation, a specialized hospital in Georgia. It had been founded by Franklin Roosevelt, President of the United States during World War II, who was also a victim of polio. I was taken to the hospital in my father's Waco plane, which I had just learned to fly. I lay helplessly on the back seat during the flight to Warm Springs.

The polio virus kills or injures nerve cells in the spine that connect the brain and voluntary muscles throughout the body. It does not kill sensory nerve cells, so my sensation was not impaired. During the following year, I had a small improvement in some nerves that were only injured.

My therapy at the hospital consisted mainly of limbering up atrophied muscles, improving the range of motion in joints, providing an arm holder that enables me to feed myself, and helping me adjust to a new lifestyle. Later Roberta and I bought a house one block from the Foundation. During the next three years, I learned to operate my life from a wheelchair.

Regaining My Self-Esteem

Not surprisingly, being crippled by polio challenged my feelings of self-esteem and security. Inside the hospital I felt all right about people seeing me in a wheelchair. But when I went out in public, I felt ashamed and embarrassed to be crippled. I thought people might perceive me as helpless, say derogatory things behind my back, or feel sorry for me or my wife.

There is a saying in personal growth circles that what you resist persists, and what you emotionally accept disappears. I was not familiar with this principle back then. Yet I somehow found a way to apply it to my handicap. After a few months of feeling self-conscious, a strategy occurred to me. I would strike back at my crippling disability *by showing myself* that I was not really disabled. I told myself that it's ability, not disability, that's really important. I started asking myself, "What can I do?"

I am unable to turn myself. I wake up every hour or two at night. In order to fall asleep again it is necessary to turn from my back to my side or vice versa. So I got busy inventing a "turnover" bed. I devised a bed that would turn me from my back to my stomach or sit me up when I pushed a switch. I discovered that it could turn two people as easily as one, and it thus worked to assist me in having a more normal sex life. The mechanism was totally safe, simple, and reliable, and I was later issued a U.S. patent on it.

This turnover bed takes the strain out of handling a paralyzed person. There are people held in nursing facilities since their families are unable to care for them because of the strength required for lifting. Using the turnover bed, even an adolescent could bathe, give full toilet assistance, and otherwise take care of a 200-pound person. I wanted to donate the patent to the Veterans Administration, hoping that many hospitalized people could once again live at home with their families. I finally got a V.A. official to look at it. He later sent me a polite letter saying that the Veterans Administration "did not buy turnover beds." I wonder if the Wright brothers were ever sent a letter from the War Department saying it did not buy airplanes! So far as I know, I'm the only handicapped person who has enjoyed this wonderful bed. The patent has expired—and I'd still like to see this invention used to help people.

I began to develop the feeling that I did not have to be so totally dependent on other people. Even though I had a crippled body, I still wanted to feel that I was a capable and lovable person.

While I was working on the turnover bed, it occurred to me that an electric wheelchair would be very handy. At that time motorized wheelchairs were not commercially available. I read in *Time* magazine about Jim Rand, who had invented an improvement in a home washing machine. I wrote to him and asked if he could make a motorized wheelchair for me. He agreed to try. A few months later he flew to Warm Springs with his precious gift, which he generously offered to me without charge. It was controlled by a single lever I could use with my right hand. After someone lifted me into the chair, I could move around on my own. My sense of independence got a big boost.

My First Book

Another part of my strategy for fighting back at polio turned out to be my writing a popular book on methods for clear thinking. For several years I had been a student of general semantics as formulated by Alfred Korzybski. I had studied with him at the Institute for General Semantics in Chicago in 1944 during a Navy furlough. I became interested in writing his biography. He visited Roberta and me in Warm Springs for two weeks, and I recorded many hours of him telling about his life and his thinking. I never got around to writing the biography, though.

Korzybski had asked himself why science was so effective. His answer was that science builds a body of knowledge based not on philosophical speculation but on rigorously testing all theories and hypotheses. In other words, science requires that careful observations tell us which ideas offer the most *predictability*. Unlike philosophy, science does not claim to be true. It simply yields reliable knowledge that helps explain and predict. No ideas are considered sacred or final; science offers the *latest* word, but never the *last* word. The method of science helps one escape from the rut of one's prejudices, comfortable notions, or the word of authority to decide which ideas apply to the real world and which can be thrown in the wastebasket.

Most people think science is created by mathematics and laboratories. Not so, he said, it's created by how we think about thinking. He noted that one of the world's greatest scientists, Charles Darwin, had never run a laboratory experiment. What had made his thinking scientific? It was his refusal to hold on to any ideas he could not prove by careful observation. Korzybski devised methods we can use with our everyday language to give increasing levels of effectiveness to our moment-to-moment thinking in business and personal life.

I decided to write a popular book on these techniques by using a dictating machine. The fingers of my right hand were just strong enough to hold a pen in a certain way that allowed me to correct the manuscript. I liked being able to do that for myself. Writing helped build my self-esteem.

When the manuscript was finished, I sent it to Harper and Row. They sent back a contract, subject only to their approval of the cartoons I planned. I wanted to add a lightness and humor to this otherwise dry subject. I had been looking around for a cartoonist who could project human feelings into common life situations. I settled on Ted Key, who was well-known for his *Saturday Evening Post* drawings of the saucy maid "Hazel," later made into a TV series. He drew 80 full-page cartoons that excellently expressed the spirit of the book. After seeing the rough sketches, Harper turned them down, but McGraw-Hill quickly accepted the book and published it in 1950 under the title *How to Develop Your Thinking Ability.* The Executives Book Club and the Semantics Book Club adopted it as a monthly selection. The Bell Telephone Company used it for training some of their top officers. We later acquired the rights from McGraw-Hill, and we now publish it under the title *Taming Your Mind.*

The Gold Coast Marathon

Gradually, I let go of my longing for things now denied me. I was beginning to realize that it was silly to long for things I couldn't do (such as playing tennis) when I didn't have enough time in the day to do the things I *could* do. I switched my time and attention to listening to my classical music collection, reading, making a turnover bed, and writing a book. My wheelchair self-consciousness was fading.

We hired two attendants on a rotating schedule to lift me and take care of my bodily needs. When the therapy was completed in 1949, Roberta, Kenny, Clara Lu, and I moved to South Miami. One of the attendants, Carl, stayed with me for about 24 years. We lived in a ranch-type home on a three-acre mango and avocado grove.

Perhaps my final way of thumbing my nose at polio was to buy a 16-foot Chris-Craft speedboat. I had eight "necking knobs" installed on the steering wheel so I could use my left elbow to turn it. It had an electric clutch I could work by moving a switch with my right hand. I decided to enter the Gold Coast Marathon, which was a 64-mile race from Miami. With Graham Miller and another friend as the crew, I raced to West Palm Beach one day and back the next morning. It was a predicted log race, which means that we picked the speed we wished to travel. We were scored on how accurately we timed our arrival at various checkpoints. I won second prize.

The following year I resolved to come in first. Based on my experience, I even more carefully calculated the speed that I would need to arrive at the checkpoints at the predicted time. In a field of about one hundred boats, I took off with two friends from Miami, raced to West Palm Beach, and returned the next day. I exuberantly crossed the finish line—and ran out of gas 15 seconds later. It turned out that I had again won second prize. But the greatest prize of all for me was that my wheelchair had disappeared! That was the last race I needed to run. I didn't *feel* crippled any more.

Creating My World

Being in a wheelchair is perhaps like having a wart on your face. While a wart is definitely visible and will be noticed by many people, the most important thing is your own *reaction* to it. If you emotionally accept having a wart on your face, it will cease to exist for you in terms of any psychological importance. When someone gets to know you, it will tend to diminish in his or her mind as well. Conversely, if you believe that everyone thinks a wart is horrible, and if you think everyone keeps looking at it, then that is probably what will happen. If you forget about the wart, and do not resist having it, others will most likely forget about it too.

I cannot reach out and take an object that someone hands me. Sometimes when I've known a person for a while, s/he will try to hand me something. Then it occurs to both of us that I can't reach for it. And we both laugh. And I feel good that s/he "forgot" I have a disability.*

I feel I can do just about anything I want from my wheelchair—especially with a little help from my friends. I find that most people are very willing to lend a hand when needed. There is usually no reason for me to hesitate to go anywhere. No matter what people do or say around me, I find that I'm not the least bit touchy in this area.

The wheelchair "disappeared" for me because I let it disappear as a concern in my life. I think that if I don't make a big deal about being crippled, no one else will either. Whether or not these statements are correct, I *believe* them to be correct. My life seems to work out *as*

---

* Please read "s/he" as "she or he."

Singing a duet
with Roberta,
1950

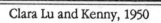

Clara Lu and Kenny, 1950

though they are true. Perhaps one's life is a self-fulfilling prophecy anyhow.

I tell myself that to a great extent we each get to create what we think is "real" and "true" in our lives. I think that polio is no longer a very important aspect of my life. It only slows me down a little bit. I see my life as having been enriched by polio—because without it, I do not think I would have discovered the personal growth methods that have meant so much to me. Perhaps I would have been so caught up in the business and social rat race that I wouldn't have sat still long enough to study my security, sensation, and power illusions—and then discover how to deal with them so I could open my heart to loving more.

My reality is that I am far too busy and involved in my life activities to have time to concern myself with self-consciousness in the wheelchair department. Today I view my so-called "handicap" as another gift my life has offered me.

Between Hurdles

Twee and my father were divorced in 1949. Since they had very different tastes and interests, it came as no surprise to me. As a young adult with my own family, I had no difficulty with their divorce; I still appreciated each of them individually. I was glad when Dad later married a wonderful woman named Polly, whom he had met about 30 years earlier.

Things perked along for me. In 1950 I was working for my father as the general manager of WMBM, a radio station he had financed. After about a year, I left to enroll at the University of Miami to complete my Bachelor of Arts degree with a major in psychology. I hoped I would learn something from the professors about living a happy life. I found out they didn't know much more about that than I did.

During this time, I operated a small real estate office from my home, specializing in acreage investments and commercial real estate. I wrote an article on growth trends in the Miami area, which got published in the *Miami Herald* real estate section. Suddenly, brokers began contacting me to find good buys for their larger investment clients. Although I only had a two-room office that I had built in the avocado grove adjoining my home, the sales skyrocketed.

The sense of security my mother had given me had withstood the polio test. My mind had avoided becoming trapped in the illusion that I was a victim of polio and was fated to live an unhappy, deprived, tragic life. However, I really got snagged on the next challenge sent my way. While I was good at using my rational mind, I had much to learn about the human heart. It took me many years to learn the next lesson my life was giving me.

3

The Bonita Experience

In the first 15 years of our marriage, Roberta and I had planned and built two homes and remodeled the one in Warm Springs. In 1956 we moved to a fourth home we had built on the Coral Gables waterway. I was successfully making money, selling large acreage investments in the rapidly growing South Florida area, and I was developing the Perrine Shopping Center in a Miami suburb. I had long dreamed of having an oceangoing yacht on which I could comfortably travel through the sparkling waters of the Bahamas and Cuba. In 1956 Roberta and I traded some property for the *Caprice*, a luxurious 71-foot vessel we docked at our waterway home.

We were married for 18 years. For the first nine years the warmth and love in our marriage steadily increased. It slowly deteriorated in the last nine. Roberta and I drifted further and further apart. We became less able to resolve our disagreements. Among other things, I considered her too inconsistent in disciplining our children; she considered me too rigid. We couldn't find the middle ground. She would often fall asleep about a half hour after supper; I usually liked to do things together in the evening and made a big deal out of her drifting off. I felt that after working all day, I should have someone to have fun with at night. I occasionally saw other women but was never emotionally involved—she wasn't supposed to know, but I'm sure she did. I had no understanding of how to deal with our differences. We played out our 18-year drama of coming together and breaking apart as innocent pawns in the grip of clashing motivations and parenting models. I didn't know how to do it any other way.

We separated. I took the *Caprice* to the Dinner Key Marina in Coconut Grove and moved aboard. One day, my attendant told me he had seen Roberta walking on the dock toward the boat when she noticed that I was talking with another woman on the bow. She stopped still, turned around, and walked away. From that time on, I found her difficult to work with in matters concerning the children.

When we were divorced in 1959, we divided up our property. She took our waterway home in Coral Gables, and I got the *Caprice* and made it my home for the next 15 years. Our children were in their teen years and we shared the child support. She was comfortable doing this for she had inherited stock in her family-owned company that makes Magic Chef stoves. My involvement with Kenny and Clara Lu fell to holiday visits and occasional trips with their school friends to the Bahamas. I felt that Roberta's bitterness influenced them against me. I didn't think I could win against Roberta's animosity, and I stopped trying. Clara Lu's judgmentalness toward me seemed to continue until many years later when Living Love helped me reach out to her.

For the next five years I had my office aboard the *Caprice*. I continued specializing in spotting growth trends and selling property to investors and home builders in the booming Miami suburbs. I also wrote a book on how good nutrition can put more life into one's years and more years into one's life. One of its innovations was a vitamin-mineral index that gave a numerical value for each food, based on the ratio of calories to vitamins and minerals. For example, white sugar had a V-M index of 0; oranges with their abundance of vitamin C scored 27. To make the book scientifically up-to-date, I took nutrition courses at the University of Miami. It was published by Frederick Fell under the title *How to Live Longer— Stronger—Slimmer*.

Around 1964, I resumed working for my father in a company he set up to sell large properties to foreign investors. During the years after my divorce from Roberta, I had several relationships that came and went as I bachelored on the *Caprice*. And then I met Bonita. Bonita was the only child of two Miami schoolteachers. She was capable of deep levels of communication, caring, and commitment. For me, she was chemistry and electricity combined. Within a few weeks, she and her young daughter, Deena, were spending every weekend with me aboard the *Caprice*. Bonita and I delighted in being together. We were married after five months.

She was about 28 years old when we were married. I was 44. She wanted a very close relationship with her life partner. That also met my models of what I wanted. As I see it, my feelings of love (as opposed to feelings of

Bonita

friendship) are powerfully generated when two things happen: First, a person has characteristics that I deeply like but that I do not have in myself; and second, she puts me in touch with parts of myself that I like.

Bonita must have been a master at giving me both experiences, for I fell rapidly in love with her, more intensely than I had ever known possible. It was Bonita who first put me in touch with the incredible power of love. During our five-month courtship and the first months of our marriage, I could not be with her enough.

I looked forward to weekends when we could be together all the time. We loved to go out in the *Caprice*, traveling to Bimini, Nassau, and the intriguing Exuma Islands. I was the captain and she became a skillful helmsperson. Her erotic skills were so perfect for me that sex generally occurred every day or every other day. At that time I was writing a book with Jacque Fresco exploring what the world of the next century may have in store for us. Bonita was fascinated by my adventures in the world of knowledge—and this helped to put me in touch with a part of myself that I liked.

The Green-Eyed Monster

During our courtship and the first few months of our marriage, it was like heaven on earth. And then life gave me an opportunity for growth. About once a week Bonita would become depressed for no reason that I could understand. She would wear a long face and become critical.

She would also make herself jealous whenever the possibility of feminine competition presented itself. I did not sneak around, and at no time was I sexually unfaithful during the period of our courtship or marriage. However, both of us knew that my ego was still mentally shopping in the sensation supermarket. Even though we shared what for me was the ultimate in sexual pleasure, my mind would still search for sexual variety— at least in my imagination. Each female that met my models would be imaginatively stripped and explored, even though I made no overt moves. And Bonita was tuned-in to me intuitively.

I would make silent calculations in which low marks would be given, for example, to any woman married to a six-foot hunk; high marks were awarded to any single lady who wore tight fitting clothes and looked at me with big, open eyes that could be hunting for something to do in the evenings.

Bonita knew I would have welcomed a sexual evening with Barbara, with whom I had previously been in a relationship. This never actually took place, because I did not want to give Bonita a factual basis for her possessiveness and jealousy.

As I look back, I can see that I was monogamous on the outside and non-monogamous on the inside. And because I wasn't actually doing what she was afraid of, I was unwilling to acknowledge the pain she felt. At that time I was more concerned about being "right" than with the compassion that comes from the heart.

My Unskillful Response to Jealousy

These sexual games of the mind set me up for an intense jealousy drama. Barbara had two children, Kathy and Steve, approaching their teen years. As a Christmas gift the year before I met Bonita, I had given them a subscription to *Reader's Digest*. A few months after Bonita and I were married, *Reader's Digest* sent me an invitation to repeat my gift at this yuletide season, and it specifically listed Kathy and Steve. When Bonita opened the mail and saw the names of Barbara's children, her jealousy clouded up and rained all over.

Since I was totally innocent in my actions (as opposed to what I was telling myself inside), I played the situation for all it was worth. I rationally pointed out that the Christmas renewal promotion was based on last year's subscription, which had happened before I even met Bonita. I righteously responded with irritation, hurt, and resentment. I questioned whether we should be together. My mind played the "right-wrong" game to the hilt. I thought inside, "How dare you unjustly accuse me! Just for that, I'm going to take my love back until you say you're sorry." Such a game can be as futile as a child holding his breath to get what he wants.

I wanted her to learn that her jealousy was unfair, unfounded, and that she "should" never be jealous toward me again unless I was sexually involved with someone. I did my best to convince her that this unwarranted jealousy of hers was an irrational attack on her loving husband, who (at least in this instance) was pure as driven snow. I wondered why she couldn't see the halo around my head!

But she was in no mood to tune-in to Saint Ken. We carried on this juicy little drama for days—with me getting increasingly righteous and determined that I would not live with her jealousy. She continued to feel more and more misunderstood by me. As I now look back on this episode, my rational mind knew that I was absolutely right, and any court in the land would uphold my innocence. Yet my heart quietly watched me treating her in an unfeeling, rational way. Today I find it incredible that I could be so totally caught in this self-defeating behavior. We probably could have both laughed together within minutes after opening the *Reader's Digest* solicitation had it not been for the unskillful way I responded.

Today my Living Love methods would enable me to respond to such jealousy by emotionally accepting it and not being defensive—I would just increase my expression of love. I now view jealousy as a passing storm on the ocean of life that I would not resist. I'd lovingly and patiently give it time to blow itself out.

I am deeply appreciative that an old dog can be taught new tricks. Flashing ahead of my story a bit, Penny, my future wife, made herself jealous early in our relationship when I was working with a talented student in one of our personal growth trainings. I did not use the situation to point out how innocent I was. I trusted that she knew this as well as I. I didn't try to talk her out of the jealousy. Instead I just emotionally accepted the way she was experiencing jealousy in the moment. I reached out and put my arm around her and genuinely expressed my love for her. I told myself that we could use the incident to increase the level of trust and love between us. All I had to do was to just love her—simply love her.

I now tell myself that love is the only oil that can eliminate the grinding of our emotional gears. Without the energy of unconditional love, it is difficult for a relationship to survive the individual diversity that constantly triggers conflict when our hearts want to love—

yet our egos are caught up in angrily defending "territorial rights."

More Jealousy Stuff

In repeated incidents, Bonita and I strongly argued about her jealousy. Since this was a major factor in my deciding to get out of the marriage, I want to share one other incident of the kind in which I solidified my notion of how "right" I was and how "wrong" Bonita was.

We were invited by our friends Hank and Jean for dinner one evening. I was deep into writing *Looking Forward* with Jacque Fresco. I began to share with Hank and Jean our fascinating predictions of the great things we felt were evolving to improve human life in the 21st century.

Hank got busy fixing supper and Jean sat on the couch soaking up every word. Bonita sat in a chair facing us getting more jealous by the minute. Although I picked up the signs, I made it a point to be even more entertaining and charming with Jean. I told myself that I was just responding in a friendly way to her request for more information about the book I was writing. I did not realize it at the time, but I orchestrated the entire event myself. Instead of playing down my conversation with Jean after I realized Bonita was jealous, I chose to antagonize her by continuing. I again cast myself in the role of unjustly accused, absolutely innocent victim of Bonita's unfounded jealousy.

Needless to say, this furnished a topic of discussion for Bonita and me on the way home and afterward. I kept myself trapped in defending my "rights." I totally justified my actions as normal for a guest to respond to the questions of the hostess. I know today that I let this clash diminish the love in my heart—and perhaps in Bonita's.

As clever as I was, I couldn't see that loving and demanding do not go together. They are like a seesaw: when loving is high, demanding is low. When demanding is high, loving is low.

The Flickering of Love

During our courtship and the first half of our marriage, I had deeply felt love for Bonita and had constantly said those three wonderful words "I love you." One morning, in the seventh month of our marriage, I woke up and realized that it had been about a month since I had said "I love you" to Bonita. I still felt love for her and I still wanted to be with her. It hit me that I had stopped verbally expressing love to her. Amazing!

Then I set myself up for another one of life's lessons. I decided that my unconscious mind which had made me stop saying "I love you" was giving me a profound message: Perhaps Bonita and I should not continue to be married. Today I still believe my unconscious withholding of those three words was giving me a profound message—and I'm equally sure that the message was *not* what I then thought it was.

I now regard such situations as a gift of the universe offering me a lesson for my inner work and growth. Life was really telling me I should let go of demanding that my partner be different from the way she was. My demands were killing the love in my heart. However, at that time it never occurred to me to let go of my unrealistic demands that my partner never be jealous without a basis I felt was justified. I was stuck in maintaining my righteous position that "I am fair, reasonable, and right; Bonita is unfair, irrational, and wrong." The best my mind could do was to view it as a way Bonita had to change for me to live happily with her.

When I asked Bonita to give me a divorce about a year after we were married, I was wholeheartedly able to say, "I love you, but I do not want to live with your jealousy and depression for the rest of my life." I did not realize that I was far too touchy in these areas. I was blinded by my tunnel vision.

This wonderful woman reluctantly and generously agreed to dissolve our marriage. On the outside, she bore up well; but I know today that on the inside she felt hurt and misunderstood. At one point she said, "I can't win no matter what I do." At the time I interpreted that as her agreeing I was right. Today I realize it was she who was right. My demands kept me boxed into creating issues in which *no one* could win.

I sometimes wonder whether the painful experience of playing out my rational stuff with Bonita was essential to my continued growth in learning the lessons my life was offering me. I think the answer is "yes." The intensity of the pain eventually got through my hard head that I needed more skill in creating and maintaining a loving relationship. But I did not yet understand how to increase my skill.

4

Benefits of
a Broken Heart

When I asked Bonita for a divorce, I thought my life would feel lighter, since I would no longer be living with someone who was sometimes depressed and jealous. I felt I'd tried my best to make our marriage work—*and I had*—given the limitations of my unskillful mental habits that made me so reactive to her jealousy and depressions.

The Jabbing Pain

It was back to the single life—hopefully free of everything I didn't like. However, I was still operating without much understanding of the enormous power of love. The idea of a "broken heart" had always seemed to me a handy cliché for writers to use in creating interesting plots. I didn't know what it felt like.

I had thought it would be easy to leave her. But after separating from Bonita, my mind was constantly preoccupied with the joys we had shared in creating the delightful events in our relationship. I soon discovered how much my heart was attached to life with her.

My mind constantly went back to the beautiful times we had shared together: boating in the Bahamas, enjoying the company of friends, and most particularly just being together, nurturing and loving each other. Every time I thought of her, which was many times each hour, I could feel a stabbing pain—an actual shooting pain in my heart. While driving around the city, whenever I saw a three-light configuration like the one on the back of the Chevrolet Bonita owned, that jabbing pain would hit me again.

I've heard that some of the greatest poetry has been written by poets who are suffering from unfulfilled love. Although I was lacking in experience, I began to do watercolor and tempera paintings. I made up in quantity what I lacked in quality; within a few months I turned out hundreds of paintings, varying in size from very small to 4 x 6 feet. I felt less pain when I had a brush in my hand. After a while I sold some to Burdine's, a local department store. My highest moment occurred when an Italian art collector bought six of my abstract tempera paintings.

Bonita bought a twin-mast sailboat and docked it on the pier just north of mine. From the stern of the *Caprice*, I could see her in her red bikini lounging on the *Stay Free* as she named it. This misery went on month after month. I told myself that the most wonderful thing that could happen in my life would be to go at least 24 hours without once thinking of Bonita. It wasn't happening, though.

After about six months of the greatest suffering I'd ever experienced, a strategy occurred to me. I would make a list of all the reasons why I did not want to

Painting aboard the *Caprice*, 1967

continue the marriage with Bonita. It consisted of several items with jealousy and depression topping the list. I made three copies, one for my desk at home, one for my office desk, and another to be kept in my pocket for instant use wherever I was. When the pain hit, I grabbed for the list.

I found that by slowly reading this list, my mind would access why I had asked for the divorce. I found the pain would begin to diminish within a few seconds. As soon as it disappeared, I quit reading the list or even thinking about it. I knew that if my mind stayed preoccupied with separating thoughts, it would risk crystallizing into hatred. I didn't want to hate her. I wanted to love her even though the way in which I expressed love and caring was feeble and flawed. One day, more than a year later, I realized I had indeed gone 24 hours without thinking of her. My broken heart was mending.

Bonita's Generosity

I'd like to share one further chain of events that happened with Bonita. I had moved to California and we'd had no contact for almost a decade. One day she and her husband, Jerry, dropped by the center I had founded in Berkeley (more about that later) and popped into my office to surprise me. She was wearing a blond wig over her black hair. I failed to recognize her. When we got that straightened out, I told her about the personal growth methods I was using in my own life and teaching others. I enjoyed being with her and her husband, and catching up on what was happening in our lives.

The following year, she and Jerry traveled to Atlanta to take a weekend workshop I was giving. In 1977 they took another personal growth workshop with me in Miami. I had just signed a contract to purchase a large training center in Kentucky from the Catholic Church, and at the workshop I put out an appeal for donations. During a break, Bonita came to me and said she wanted to donate all of the settlement she had received from our divorce to the purchase of our new center! My mind suddenly flashed on the incredible miracles that happen as I learn to love unconditionally. And I felt humbly appreciative of this noble act by this beautiful lady.

A few months later, Bonita came back to the center in Berkeley and took our one-month training. Then Jerry flew out to take a week-long training with her. At that time, I was in a relationship with a woman named Lenore and I purposely avoided any energy that would have given confusing messages to her or to Lenore—or to my own mind. She later visited our center in Kentucky and would sometimes drop by to see me when I visited in Miami.

I did not hear from her for about five years; then I received the message that she had died of cancer. My heart wished that I had really been there for her—both during our marriage and during her battle with cancer. And I honored her choice not to contact me in her last months. Perhaps this would have brought up memories of the rise and fall of our marriage that could have increased her pain.

No Pain—No Gain

I find it awesome to reflect that today in minutes I could probably resolve inside myself the issues that caused the breakup of both of my marriages—just by using the Living Love methods I found later in my life.

There is a saying in the personal growth field: "No pain, no gain." I tell people in my seminars that we all create the "soap opera" that is perfect for our growth.* However, we must *choose* to take the growth. I find that when I ignore a lesson, life just keeps giving me the same message again but with increasing pain until I take notice. The quicker I learn the lesson, the less the pain. My ego is often adept at protecting its current mental habits, attitudes, and values from the lessons life is trying to give me. Sometimes my ego has been like a turtle that is fortified behind its built-in fortress of right-wrong, good-bad, and fair-unfair judgments. It forgets the adage, "Every way of a person is right in his or her own mind."

I know that Bonita and I had together created the experiences we both needed most for our next steps in personal growth. Often when people have created a broken heart for themselves, they pick what I consider to be the wrong lesson such as "love is dangerous," "women (or men) are not to be trusted," or "I'll never fall in love again—at least not completely."

I'm glad I didn't fall into any of these cynical traps. Bonita helped me go from freshman to sophomore in the "University of Living Love." Like all sophomores, I still had much to learn.

* I use "soap opera" to help us perceive the daily drama of our lives from a mountaintop perspective. Viewing one's life as a soap opera helps us gain added insight on the events in our lives with less self-centered bias. It helps us laugh at ourselves and not take life so seriously.

5

The Lure of Money

What is the surest and most dependable way to be happy? What is it that almost everyone is running after? My ego thought it knew the answer. It was *money*. I not only thought it was the answer to feeling secure in life; it would also be handy for increasing my sensations and power—a triple whammy!

During my teens and twenties, I felt sure that if I had enough money, I could be happy. If I wanted love or sex, a woman would be attracted to me because of wealth. If I wanted cars, boats, or fine sound equipment, money was obviously the only answer. My illusion was that wealth not only brought self-esteem, it also sucked in the esteem of just about everyone else. Money was a stable, effective basis for personal security and happiness. Money was IT!

The Young Entrepreneur

The illusion of money as the basis of my security and happiness led me into quite a waltz over the years. I was blessed with a father who did not hand me much money. However, he gave me lots of opportunities to earn it. Even when I was in elementary school, I remember working for 25¢ an hour in my father's business using a rubber stamp on envelopes and letterheads. In my junior high school days, I worked on Saturdays in the printing department of his real estate business. I learned to operate the mimeograph, multigraph, and address-ograph, to set movable type, and to perform other skills of a printer. When the head of the department left, I ran the printing machines for a number of months until a replacement was found.

During high school I learned to operate a photo lab that my father set up in the basement of our home. I arranged for two afternoon study periods, and I got a note from my father asking that I permanently skip them. I would get out of school at 1:40. I then used a family car to take photos of homes and other properties needed for my father's growing real estate business. At night I would process them and turn out 5 x 7-inch photographs for 15¢ each. Even at these low prices, my monthly gross usually ran between $100 and $200—a good sum for a teenager doing part-time work in those days. I used this money to buy classical phonograph records and maintain my 16-foot sailboat.

When I drove to Duke University in Durham, North Carolina, I packed my entire photo lab into the back seat. I rented an upstairs space from a local photographer. I was able to continue making money through portrait photography, publishing a 1940 Duke University calendar, and working for two summers at Camp Dixie for Boys in Wiley, Georgia as camp photographer.

The *Caprice*, 1965

A Nationwide Business

Although I was active in real estate in South Florida for many years, my drive for money perhaps reached its fullest flowering around 1968 when I set up a company selling real estate investments nationwide. I had qualified for a brokerage license in Florida and had learned how to analyze investments by working in my father's business.

My new company was based on the premise that it doesn't take much more work to sell a big property and earn a big commission than to sell a small property and make a small commission. Outside of Miami, I only brokered properties valued at one million dollars or more. This insured that the minimum commission would be $50,000—a five percent sales fee. The company operated nationwide specializing in the sale of income-producing properties such as shopping centers, apartment complexes, and large office buildings.

I got copies of the tax rolls of major cities such as Dallas, Atlanta, Birmingham, and Jacksonville. To find properties for sale, I used automatic typing machines to grind out letters to the owners of properties with a tax assessment of at least a million dollars. Through trade magazines, I also researched the names of major investors who were buying the larger properties.

Then the game was to put the buyers and sellers together.* My father had shown me how to write a

---

* The word "game" has several meanings. Eric Berne in *Games People Play* describes many "dishonest" personality games. Throughout this book, I'll use "game" with another meaning. "Game" will nonjudgmentally refer to a life activity as in "I'm in the insurance game" or "I play the wheelchair game." *Anything* can be played as a game. The concept of "game" helps me regard any life activity as a challenge, an adventure, or sport—not a serious, cliff-hanging problem.

booklet giving a detailed description of each property, complete with pictures, floor plans, and other details needed by an experienced investor. My company secured listings nationwide, wrote up the property booklets, and mailed them by the dozens to investors who were making major real estate purchases. The results were phenomenal. During the first calendar year of its operation, the firm had a gross sales volume of $25 million. This escalated to $32 million during its second year. I put the profits back into expanding the business instead of paying myself a big salary.

The Failure of My Success

And yet, in spite of all this outstanding success, I increasingly experienced that I was not getting what I most wanted in my life—deep feelings of heart-to-heart love and peace of mind. My life seemed like a rat race— a perpetual competitive scramble. I disliked treating people as pawns or as kings in the money game. After all, I told myself, we're all human beings.

I asked myself if the constant hunt for money was the way I wanted to live the rest of my life. I questioned whether this was the answer to my finding happiness in life. I wondered if real happiness was possible—minute by minute, day by day, year by year?

I had thoroughly hunted for inner feelings of security. I had tried parental approval. I had received applause for my success in the money game from friends and business associates. Like the shoes in a showcase, they look fine on display. But how do they work when you buy them? The shoe may look great, yet only the wearer knows where it rubs his foot raw.

Getting along with others, achievement, and financial comfort are desirable aspects of a well-rounded life. Yet I found they were not giving me the deepest feelings of inner peace. They were like desert mirages that seem to promise water if the thirsty traveler can only get there. And when the destination is reached, the promise of water is always somewhere else. Many talented, achieving people, like my mother, feel insecure inside even though they lead successful lives. Many wealthy people constantly feel financially threatened because they're afraid their money may be heavily taxed, stolen, or lost in the stock market. When played gently and lovingly, money is just another game of life. When we worry about it and cling to it as our security blanket, it sets us up for unhappiness.

Personal growth usually comes most rapidly when *nothing* appears to be working in our lives—or when *everything* seems to be working and we're still not happy. We need a jolt to get out of the rut we're in—to try something new. We have to be open to finding "new" answers to old problems. Auntie Mame was talking about me when she flippantly said, "Life is a banquet and most poor suckers are starving to death." On the outside my soap opera looked great; on the inside it felt unsatisfactory.

Was this IT? Is this what life is all about? Can life be more than a constant clawing for security, sensation, and power in the form of money, sex, prestige, pride, and control? I wondered how I could find genuine love and happiness.

My search for how to make my life work better also made me a frequent shopper in the sensation center just down the road from the security center. Its many gifts came wrapped in such attractive packages! Did playboys and playgirls have the answer to a happy life? Maybe this was IT!

Part II

Seeking Happiness
Through Sensations

6

Sensational Stuff

When I was six I thought that happiness would be mine if I could just get enough ice cream cones. The second ice cream cone that I sometimes wheedled from my parents did nothing to dispel this illusion. One day when I was able to finance it (ice cream cones cost a nickel each in those days), I had my third, fourth, and fifth—all within a few minutes. Although my fortune of 50¢ enabled me to explore the outer reaches of ice cream pleasuredom, I found that my appetite was satiated— and I felt queasy. If one cone is pleasurable, I found that five cones are not five times more enjoyable!

To insure the survival of the species, nature builds in strong urges for food and sex. This seems to work well for most animals. Unfortunately the human mind is able to turn the desire for sensations into dimensions that may sometimes reduce one's overall enjoyment of life—and often shorten one's life span. The pleasures of calories and orgasms can sometimes carry too high a price tag. I've had much to learn about wisely balancing the games of life that are motivated by pleasurable sensations.

Shirley on the *Caprice*, 1970

After I broke up my marriage with Bonita, I began to play out my sensation desires as a 45-year-old affluent bachelor living on a large yacht on Biscayne Bay. My life was giving me the opportunity to fully explore these compulsions in my search for happiness.

This was to be my predominant and longest personal growth challenge: the pursuit of pleasure, love, and validation through sexual relationships. For some of us, our greatest lessons are in the area of security and self-esteem. For others like myself, they lie in the sensation area. For some, the major growth will involve power, pride, or prestige. In descending order of importance, I realize today that my own happiness depended on breakthroughs in sensation, power, and, least of all, security.

I think the early programming given by my mother, and my father's model of self-assurance, enabled me to skip the doubts about self-worth that plague many people. So I was free to get stuck in sensation stuff—and stuck I was for many, many years. A lot of the reason for taking so long to get unstuck was that I didn't know I was stuck—and even if I had known, I wouldn't have known what to do to help myself.

Shirley

My next significant relationship was with Shirley. She was tall with red hair, bright eyes, and a ready smile. She was deeply loving and caring. Her social conscience led her to visit black neighborhoods, helping people register for elections. From the beginning of our relationship, I told her I was not interested in a one-to-one commitment; I'd had enough of marriage. That was okay with her—she said she was not looking for that either. I made it clear that I would date other people—and would always be honest about what I was doing. She said that every Wednesday she had a sexual date with a longtime office friend and, like me, she did not want jealousy and possessiveness. We unknowingly set up a divided game, behind it all wanting deeper levels of togetherness and commitment—and both running away from it at the same time.

Shirley introduced me to Dottie and John. They had been childhood sweethearts, were married, and now had two adolescent children, Guy and Jill. We all became very close friends. Shirley and I were aware that Dottie and John were deeply committed to each other and to their marriage—and yet each had outside sexual relationships they kept hidden from the other. Since Shirley and I had arrived at an agreement of permissiveness and honesty in our relationship, we wondered why these two wonderful people who were so loving and devoted should have secret lives and not share everything with each other.

We decided to urge them to be honest with each other about their sexual interests outside of their marriage. Thus encouraged, Dottie and John began to talk to each other about their affairs. An enormous jealousy flared up. For a week, we were worried they might not stay together. To our relief, the love in their hearts overrode their differences—and they worked things out.

For years after that, Dottie and John's relationship seemed ideal to me. They had evolved to eliminate the mental habits of jealousy and possessiveness. They gave each other complete freedom. And yet they had a 20-year marriage with solid levels of communication, caring, and commitment.

My desire to combine heart-to-heart togetherness with the spice and variety of non-monogamy threw me off the track for years. I did my best to reproduce it in my life, and yet I could never get it to work for me for long. Although I could get agreements (as with Shirley) to maintain a primary relationship that was open to other secondary sexual relationships, there always seemed to be certain fundamental objections in the minds of my partners—even though they had verbally agreed not to be possessive. And I was slow to recognize this contradiction. I kept trying and trying—and my relationships kept dissolving and dissolving. The small quiet voice of my inner wisdom was still being drowned out by the insistence of my sexual appetite. And then in the summer of 1970 my life gave me new clues that began to pull me out of the rut I was in.

7

Exploring
New Horizons

Early in 1970, Shirley, with whom I'd been in a relationship for several years, was fed up with her boss at the insurance company branch where she was office manager. She had been to Esalen Institute in Big Sur, California and was attracted to the new viewpoints she had come in touch with. Although she did not like leaving her friends, she moved to San Francisco.

I was still living aboard the *Caprice* at the Dinner Key Marina. To meet people, every Sunday night I had a musical gathering with an open invitation to anyone who wished to enjoy two hours of recorded classical music aboard the *Caprice*. In June, when I was about six months away from my 50th birthday, life presented me with a series of experiences that eventually showed me how to enormously increase my inner peace and happiness.

Baptism at Esalen

I had read a *Life* magazine article about the Esalen Institute at Big Sur, California. Esalen offers many excellent personal growth programs. Overlooking the Pacific Ocean, it has natural hot baths which both sexes use together without bathing suits. Psychology and sex were two of my favorite interests. I thought Esalen would provide me with both. I enrolled for two week-long workshops: one on Gestalt training and the other on improving relationships.

I had learned to play my limited games of life reasonably well. The material values I tried to radiate were: author of three books, well-known businessperson, and captain and owner of a 71-foot yacht. These assets in which I took such pride in Miami seemed like liabilities in the world of Esalen. I recognized someone I had previously known in Miami and suggested we get together that evening. But he replied candidly that he didn't want to waste his time in intellectual head trips. When I recovered from the shock, I asked myself, "What is he talking about?"

The values I perceived at Esalen were: intuitive sensitivity, deeper understanding of one's motives and hang-ups, playing down sexual differences in clothing (no tight clothing to emphasize breasts), a taboo on the macho approach to sex in which the male captures the female, and tuning-in to what life has to offer right here and now (instead of being so preoccupied with past or future events).

I had hoped to create at least one sexually intimate relationship at Esalen. But I was in a world in which I just

My visit to the Esalen Institute, June 1970

didn't know the language or local customs. Yet it was a world I found intriguing and wanted to learn more about.

Jealousy Is Tricky

On my way back to Miami I spent a day with Shirley, who now had a job with the same insurance company in San Francisco. She was living with a man she had met there named John. Knowing her interest in a sexually open lifestyle while at the same time having a primary relationship with one person, I asked her how things were working out with John in this way.

She told me that from the beginning both of them had a clear agreement that they would have other sexual partners. They had met a couple who was interested in spending an evening together and exchanging partners. She and John went to their apartment, and after dinner they sat around talking and sipping wine. Then John and the other woman went into the bedroom. Shirley noticed they had disappeared. About ten minutes later, she walked into the bedroom and there they were— *flagrante delicto*.

Shirley said she immediately triggered strong feelings of jealousy, anger, insecurity, and hurt! John was having sex with the other lady—and had done it *without her knowing!*

It wasn't that Shirley had felt that John could have sex with the other woman only when she was present. Her expectation was that at some point after dinner, they would begin to caress each other, and finally sex would be shared in whatever way it happened. Shirley made herself jealous when John did what they had planned to do all along—but in a slightly different way than she had in mind.

Shirley's story was evidence to me of the incredible tenacity of our possessive mental "programs" (using a computer analogy) that make us vulnerable to insecurity and jealousy—even in situations where our rational minds have accepted non-monogamous patterns. It emphasized the importance of being aware of the some-times opposing habits of thinking that can cause the mind to be divided against itself. Her experience gave me an example of how we can think one way and simultaneously feel a contradictory way. The human mind is a very complicated device!

I was learning that the long-term success Dottie and John had in creating an open sexual relationship, with a deep level of love and intimacy, was a rare thing—it was like making a hole in one in golf. I was finally starting to perceive that my dreams of elysian fields would not translate effectively into reality with the real people in my life. And then something happened that gave me a quantum jump in my growth.

8

Getting Enough

In late summer of 1970, the Humanistic Psychology Association held its annual meeting in Miami Beach. Again a wonderful fit for my interests at that time—psychology and perhaps sexual opportunities. I temporarily moved the *Caprice* to a dock near the hotel that was the headquarters for the convention. Here for the first time I had my alpha brain waves measured and found they were favorably strong compared with beta waves. I heard a talk by a student of a Tibetan lama named Chögyam Trungpa, and I attended a workshop led by Zerka Moreno, wife of the founder of psychodrama.

A Trip on the Bay

I met Dr. Ed Elkin and three other psychotherapists. I invited them over to the *Caprice* and proposed that we spend several days together after the convention. They liked the idea. The night before we were to leave on our cruise, I realized that they planned to use psychedelics. I had thought this was a first step toward trashing one's life. However, these were successful psychotherapists,

Dr. Ed Elkin and other psychologists
after the conference, 1970

engaged in a respectable profession, and they seemed to have their lives in good order. How could this be?

They invited me to join them and I declined. As I pondered the situation, it occurred that if I ever wanted to try this, it would make sense to do so with four psychotherapists in attendance. So I told them I had changed my mind. Early the next morning I took a pill similar to peyote which is used by Native Americans in religious rites.

About a half hour after taking the small pill, I began to experience sexual orgasms without external stimulation. It was enormously pleasant. The orgasms occurred about once every 15 to 20 seconds, and they kept going—and I kept enjoying. (I later asked the others if they'd had the experience of orgasm and was informed they hadn't.) After about an hour of nonstop ecstasy, I'd had enough! They told me that there was no way to turn it off; it would diminish in a few hours.

After two hours of continuous orgasm, I found myself completely satiated and uncomfortable. Like having too many ice cream cones, *I was actually suffering from an overdose of pleasurable sensations*. The orgasms gradually decreased in intensity, and I was comfortable after about five hours. Months later I tried it again and no orgasm occurred.

I've never used the hard drugs that threaten our society today. It has now been about 15 years since I've used a mind-altering substance. I prefer to enjoy my life using psychological techniques for personal growth; I know today that such methods can help a person achieve insights without mind-altering drugs. They work much better—and they're legal.

I had received the message life was offering me. Like ice cream, sex is just another sensation. So why let it drive me so much?

Laying Down a Burden

What a lesson! From that experience of enoughness, a process was happening. Women were less and less perceived by me as sexual objects, and I was gradually letting go of the feeling that the doors of happiness open widest when I'm having sex. I still had a long way to go, however.

As my programming slowly evolved toward loving unconditionally, sex was becoming just another enjoyable game of life. I could let it happen in a flowing, unforced way instead of trying to *make* it happen. I could perceive women that I found sexually attractive as human beings like me—not as possessors of a much desired genital commodity that I had to have to be happy.

For most of my adult life, I had thought that relaxation from sexual desire could only be experienced when I was with a sexually cooperative woman. Although it took a few more years to deeply activate it, this experience on the *Caprice* unlocked the door to my understanding that it was possible to master my desires. I would later learn to turn them on or off *without repressing or ignoring my urges* as I got in touch with my internal wisdom.

That new understanding was like laying down a heavy burden that I had been carrying much of my life. The growth experience with my four friends did not instantly transform 100 percent of my previous preoccupation with sex. It was only a small part of my journey of personal growth—a growth that within three years would enable me to change most of my insistent demands ("I can't be happy unless I have it") that had pushed me for so many decades. I no longer set up my lifestyle to maximize sex. I was beginning to find that, like money, sex wasn't IT.

9

Dave and Terry

After my psychotherapist friends had departed from the *Caprice*, I noticed they had left two books on my desk. At first I thought they'd forgotten them. When I looked closely, I realized they had chosen these books for me. One was *The Book* by Alan Watts and the other was *The Master Game* by Robert de Ropp. These books told of the frontiers of the human mind in its search for higher levels of awareness, wisdom, inner peace, clarity, enjoyment, and purpose in life. At that time I had authored *How to Develop Your Thinking Ability*, and had done some graduate work in psychology. I thought I knew something about the mind. As I read the books my friends had left, I saw that my previous work was only a beginning. They pointed toward effective new ways to deal with my upset feelings of frustration, anger, and hurt.

A couple of weeks later I was in the Coconut Grove Park which adjoins the marina where I docked the *Caprice*. Coconut Grove at that time was the Greenwich Village of the Miami area. The tropical atmosphere attracted visitors on low budgets whom I called "hippies." Every evening they put together a community stew made of gleanings from the trash bins of local supermarkets plus any donations. A couple of times I'd given them a few dollars to add to the festivities. Since my visit to Esalen, I'd become more interested in learning what made these people tick.

Here I was, a 50-year-old man in a wheelchair, dressed conventionally, and living on a yacht nearby. I could hardly pass as one of the "flower children." Yet I found that my friendly interest was instantly reciprocated and I was always welcome during my intermittent visits. One evening at the park, I met Terry. She was in her twenties and wore a white dress with apparently nothing underneath. She was barefoot, wore no make-up, and had long, tousled, light brown hair. After we met, my ego trotted out the credentials that I felt would be most likely to impress her: the books I had written on the future, thinking methodology, and nutrition. As it happened, she was into health foods.

Then to my disappointment, she mentioned that she wanted me to meet her friend Dave. Dave was a lean, good-looking man in his early thirties who spoke rapidly and intensely. He had operated a health food store in St. Johnsbury, Vermont and had been with Chögyam Trungpa, the Tibetan lama.

Trungpa had come from Tibet via England earlier that year to establish a teaching center in the United States. He'd set up Tail of the Tiger in Barnet, Vermont—about 12 miles from where Dave lived. Dave had also been visiting Ram Dass, an ex-Harvard psychology professor who had spent some time in India. All of this, plus possible intimacy with Terry, led me to invite them to spend the night with me on the *Caprice*. They were living in a shabby Dodge van, and they readily accepted my invitation.

The Master Game

Because they sensed an openness in me, Dave and Terry began to play a growth game with me. They apparently said to themselves something like "Here is a man trying to make his life work by making money, living affluently on a yacht, and enticing feminine partners. His attachments to money and sex are his biggest problems—and they will probably create more and more unhappiness for him as he gets older."

Dave and Terry began to set up situations to make me aware of my addictive, demanding drives in the area of money and sex. They were testing me to find out if I could awaken to a deeper level of insight to get free of my dependence on these two fluctuating, limited ways to find happiness.

I became fascinated with Dave's nonstop output of information. He had a background in sociology, and we had a high level of rapport. I invited them to live aboard the *Caprice* as long as they were in Miami. They decided to stay since they felt they had something to give me— although at the time I hadn't the slightest idea of the enormity of their gift.

Although my deeper interest gradually shifted to the information Dave was continually offering me, I also wanted to establish a sexual relationship with Terry. She seemed to encourage me, and Dave did not object. When we were alone and I tried to touch her, she would say, "You're attached to sex, aren't you?" This question was a bit disconcerting at that strategic moment—but she insisted that I deal with it. I'd quickly reply, "No, I'm not attached to sex. I just enjoy it in a natural way." She would then do her best to help me understand that I was attached—and yet I continued to passionately deny any attachment (although I wasn't sure what she meant by "attachment").

Dave explained that when we're attached to something and aren't getting what we want, we temporarily lose our natural beauty—and we also alienate people. He defined attachment as wanting what we don't have or clinging to what we do have. He stressed that when we're no longer attached, we can feel strong on the inside and gentle on the outside. I heard the words, but so what?

As things turned out, I never even got to first base with Terry, and I finally got tired of our discussion over my attachment to sex. I now know that resistance is the normal first response when the mind has an attachment. The ego does its best to deny, hide, or protect it.

Sex and Money

Just as I stubbornly denied my attachment to sex, I also resisted Dave's attempt to give me insight into my addictive attachment to money. He obviously perceived that money was the basis of the security, sensation, and power games I was playing in life. I stoutly rationalized that, especially for a handicapped person, money was needed to live, our civilization was built on money as a medium of exchange, and that it would be most irresponsible if I did not try to financially provide for myself. He agreed that there's nothing wrong with the money game—it's just the emotional *attachment* to it that causes one's unhappiness. I still couldn't understand

Dave and Terry spoofing the guru game
at the Dinner Key Marina , 1970

what he meant by "attachment." How can you work, earn money, and not be attached to it?

We had long talks on the *Caprice* during the evenings. My attempt to understand what he was talking about was genuine, but I was thoroughly confused when he said things like "You could have a million dollars, and it's all okay, and you don't have to be attached to the million dollars. This does not mean that you give it away—or it might mean that. It's just that to live a happy life, you've got to give up the inner attachment—but not necessarily give up in daily life what you've been attached to."

I knew there was something very worthwhile and substantial in what he was trying to tell me—but I just couldn't get it. I wasn't willing to give up trying to penetrate the possible wisdom he was doing his best to explain to me. The trick was that it couldn't be taught—it had to be caught.

The Gift of the Hollywood Police

After a few weeks, I had the feeling Dave was ready to give up on me. I was too set in my ways. He and Terry got in their beat-up old van and headed north. But the sly hand of destiny intervened and they were stopped by the police in Hollywood, Florida about 18 miles north of Miami. Hollywood was upwardly mobile, tourist oriented, and tried to attract wealthy retirees. Although he was driving carefully through the city on U.S. 1, the Hollywood police were probably trying to discourage hippies with such disreputable vans from even driving through their city. Or perhaps they thought they could make a drug bust. Dave had no drugs. However, the police weren't entirely disappointed. He had lost his driver's license, and they threw him in jail for the night.

Terry came to the *Caprice* about 5:30 the next morning in tears. She explained what had happened to them. I immediately got a couple hundred in cash and headed for the Hollywood jail. When I bailed him out, he was smiling. He could hardly wait to tell us what a wonderful time he'd had in jail!

I'd expected him to be resentful, critical of Hollywood law, recoiling from the inmates he'd been incarcerated with, and needing consolation. Instead he told me about his interesting cell mates; he had apparently spent most of the night learning how they lived their lives. He saw the Hollywood police as just doing their "thing"—a bit intensely, but he wasn't feeling resentful.

He would now have to stay in Miami about two more weeks until his trial came up. I welcomed this added time with them. Dave had given me a living demonstration of what it was like to deal with a situation without attachment. Although he *preferred* not to spend the night in jail, he was not *attached* to avoiding jail. He could play the game of life in the form it was currently being offered to him—and make decisions without the separating emotions of fear, frustration, anger, resentment, irritation, or hatred. By the time the case came to trial, Dave had written to Vermont to get another driver's license which he presented to the judge. The case was dismissed. After all, he had not committed any crime.

At this point Dave and Terry began to develop the feeling that I might not be such a disappointing student after all. We went to Bimini together on the *Caprice,* and he continued to call me on the sensation and power games that I was so busy living out—that looked so successful on the outside. He didn't let me get away with anything. He would point out my attachments and the "bad vibes" they brought into my life.

Dave and Terry had been with me about two months. I guess they felt I was still too wet behind the ears to be left alone. They wanted me to have some contact with other people who were into personal growth. He suggested that we take a trip up the Eastern seaboard. I arranged to get away from my business, and we took off in my Cadillac driven by Carl, my longtime helper.

We first visited the farm of Marion Petty in western Virginia. Marion owned several hundred acres and used them in a way that did not fit into my real estate programming. Anyone who wanted to live on his land was free to do so. Folks could come and farm it, even put up a shelter or a house, and live there as long as they wanted—all at no charge. He asked that they not do anything illegal or commercial; otherwise there were no requirements.

There was a small house about half a mile from his home that was open to any people passing through. He did not furnish food, but there was a wood-burning potbellied stove for keeping warm. For the first time in my life, I slept on the floor. I made sure that someone kept the stove burning all night so the November cold could not get inside.

The Trappist Monastery

Dave also took me to a Trappist monastery in Virginia. I saw the simple "cells" where the monks slept. I had heard before that the Trappist monks used to take a vow of silence but that it had been repealed. Trying to sound knowledgeable, I said to the elderly monk who was guiding us through the monastery, "I suppose it's nice now that you can talk." The elderly man turned to me, opened his eyes wide and replied, "Oh no, it was much better when we all remained in silence."

At another point, the monk picked up a cup that had two handles. He volunteered, "Holding it with two hands makes me feel like a child."

Why would a grown man want to feel like a child? He did not explain, nor did I ask. I later decided that he was referring to the simple way that a young child usually trusts life to give what s/he needs and does not worry about the future.

We also went to a spiritual center in Connecticut. On the day we arrived, everyone was in silence; writing was permitted but no speaking. We came in the morning, stayed all day, and left in the late afternoon.

I'd been surrounded by over a dozen people who were busy doing a variety of things but who never said a word. This was quite a strange experience for me. I would occasionally write a question to someone who would write their answer. Though I didn't understand the value of this practice at the time, it seemed to fill me with a certain peace I was unaccustomed to. I decided to just sit back and enjoy myself.

As we drove away, I assessed the overall impact of being with people I could not talk to. I felt I had tuned-in to them profoundly and vividly without conversing. Strangely, the lack of auditory input had not been a handicap; it had actually been an advantage in fully being there and receiving what was happening! I had insight into deeper intuitive dimensions of life—ones often lost when we spray the panorama of our lives with our stream of words and ideas.

Dave and Terry left soon after we returned to Miami. But I was changed. I could never return to a life motivated primarily by money and sex.

I had tasted sweeter fruits, and I was determined to experience the real cornucopia of life that I now knew was possible: more energy, more insight, more love, more joy, more inner peace, and a feeling of purpose in life. I remembered Dave telling me about the Tibetan lama. I registered for his 1970 Christmas seminar.

Part III
My Gradual Awakening

10

The Turning Point

About two weeks before my trip to Vermont, Shirley phoned from San Francisco. She told me she would be in Miami during Christmas week. Perhaps we could take a trip to Bimini with our friends Dottie and John?

Shirley and I had been intimate for three years before she moved to the West, and she had even taken an apartment in Coconut Grove near the marina so it was easy for us to be together. Although I had been with others, I had not found anyone to replace Shirley in my life since she had left earlier that year. After hanging up, I remembered that I had registered for the Christmas workshop with the lama.

This was a real dilemma. Which should I choose: a long-desired weekend filled with pleasure and companionship, or an opportunity to increase my wisdom in areas that could change my life? Well, I thought, I could always take a later seminar with the lama. "Are these the values I most want in my life?" I asked myself. "Wouldn't it be wiser to put the highest priority on my growth, and

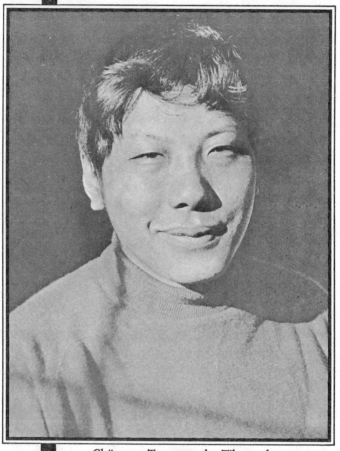

Chögyam Trungpa, the Tibetan lama,
at Tail of the Tiger, 1970

then trust my life to give me enough companionship and pleasure?"

I called Shirley back and explained the situation to her. She agreed to come a day earlier and stay a day after I returned from Vermont. The day and night we had together before I flew to Vermont were precious. I liked bringing her up to date on the adventures I'd been having in the last six months since my trip to Esalen in June. She appreciated the new developments that were happening in my life.

Tail of the Tiger

On Christmas I flew to Boston with a helper. We rented a car and headed for Barnet, Vermont. I was delighted by the soft white snow adorning the trees and the long icicles hanging from the eaves of the houses— quite a novelty for a Miamian. Tail of the Tiger was a two-story white farmhouse with the front entrance painted bright red. The snow around the house was two to three feet deep.

I had told myself, "When in Rome do as the Romans do." A few weeks back, I had bought some native clothes imported from India. Although I didn't use them, I wore meditation beads around my neck. It turned out that I was the weirdest dressed person in the entire place. Everyone else was dressed casually just like other people in the Vermont winter. How could I have been so foolish? The message: Do not get so caught up in the form that I substitute outer trappings for genuine humility and spirituality.

On the first night we were all seated at the dinner table when the Tibetan lama came downstairs to join us. Based on the movie *Lost Horizon*, I had an illusion of what a high spiritual being was like—austere, wizened, and detached from the world. Chögyam Trungpa destroyed any such models. He was in his twenties and had been in an automobile accident. He hobbled in and was soon talking with people, drinking a can of beer, and munching on a large turkey leg. His actions were a clear statement that spirituality lies not in rigid models of behavior. Instead it consists of living truth.

As I got to know him better, I realized that he personified the awareness described by the Third Patriarch of Zen:

> *When thought is in bondage the truth is hidden,*
> *for everything is murky and unclear*
> *and the burdensome practice of judging*
> *brings annoyance and weariness. . . .*
> *What benefit can be derived*
> *from distinctions and separations? . . .*
> *To set up what you like*
> *against what you dislike*
> *is the disease of the mind. . . .*
> *When the mind exists undisturbed in the Way,*
> *nothing in the world can offend,*
> *and when a thing can no longer offend,*
> *it ceases to exist in the old way.*

The Noble Truths

One morning while I was browsing in the library at Tail of the Tiger, I picked up a book about Buddha. Buddha clearly stated he was a man, not a god. The book explained that the huge statues around the Buddhist shrines in Asia may be misleading to most Westerners. He is revered, it said, as a human being that achieved the ultimate in personal growth as defined by seven characteristics: mindfulness (awareness), wisdom, energy, rapture, tranquility, concentration, and equanimity.

Buddha was the son of King Suddhodana in the sixth century B.C., in the area now known as Nepal. He gave himself the life mission of discovering what causes human happiness and unhappiness. He went beyond surface appearances to the most profound psychological depths. When he finally discovered the answers sitting under a bodhi tree, he boiled them down to several "noble truths." Here in the wintery setting with the Tibetan lama, they acquired a deep significance for me.

The first noble truth stated that all life is suffering. That didn't make sense to me. I don't suffer all the time, and neither do others. Normally I would have stopped right there and put the book down. But something urged me to read on. I began to understand that it doesn't mean we suffer all the time. It means that our lives—including those of our husbands, wives, children, friends, bosses, workers, and the state of the world—will never fit all the demands in our heads so that we can enjoy our lives continuously.* We're constantly vulnerable to such negative feelings as fear, disappointment, frustration, anger, and resentment. When that moment of happiness does dawn, it doesn't remain. Our minds continually jerk us up and down between happiness and unhappiness. Seldom do we stay really happy for long. Sometimes life throws situations at us that result in unhappiness for days, weeks, months, or even years. The first noble truth described the *predicament* we're all in.

---

*DEMAND or ADDICTIVE DEMAND: A programming or operating instruction in the mind that makes me upset or unhappy if it is not satisfied. A desire that I think I must have to feel happy. Wants and desires are demands if they trigger such emotions as fear, frustration, or anger when I don't get what I want. For example, "My programming demands that I not get caught in a traffic jam."

In the meditation room at Tail of the Tiger, 1970

The second noble truth diagnosed the *cause* of our predicament. Attachments, it said, are the cause of all our unhappiness. I thought back to what Dave and Terry had tried to tell me but which my ego had refused to apply in my life. I began to understand that our conscious and unconscious attachments and demands subtly work to set up where we live, what we do, what we notice, what we think, how we feel, how we interact with other people—and even how we experience ourselves!

The book revealed to me Buddha's profound psychological insight that it's not us, or how people around us are behaving, or the state of the world that makes us feel unhappy. It's the models in our heads—our unconscious beliefs, our demands, our expectations, our hangups, our insistent desires—that create the experience of unhappiness. It's not even our minds—it's the mental habits our minds have picked up. Buddha understood about the "programs" of the mind 2,500 years before the computer age!*

The third noble truth told me *how to solve* this problem—how to break out of my self-imposed box. To get rid of suffering and unhappiness, it said, get rid of attachments.† I was seeing that I could just alter my mental programming that was keeping me vulnerable to unhappiness. Other people didn't have to change for me to be happy. My mind raced through scenes from the

* For a modern review by Dr. Daniel Goleman of Harvard of the work of this pioneering psychologist exploring the human potential, see: Daniel Goleman, "The Buddha on Meditation and States of Consciousness, Part I: The Teachings," *The Journal of Transpersonal Psychology*, 4, No. 1 (1972), pp. 1-44; and Daniel Goleman, "The Buddha on Meditation and States of Consciousness, Part II: A Typology of Meditation Techniques," *The Journal of Transpersonal Psychology*, 4, No. 2 (1972), pp. 151-210.

† Buddha formulated a fourth noble truth—the "eight-fold path," which spells out how to get rid of attachments. The Living Love system represents a modern version for personal growth.

past in which I had felt miserable when someone didn't meet my expectations: Roberta falling asleep at night, Bonita feeling jealous and depressed, Terry refusing to have sex with me. I saw from this point of clarity that it was my *programming* that had caused my unhappiness—not their behavior—and I could *change* my programming.* That must be a lot easier to do than changing *them*. Heaven knows I had tried that!

It was falling into place. I could let go of my emotional demands and still play the game of trying to get others to change when they didn't do and say what I wanted them to. The key was my learning not to feel upset if they didn't change the way I wanted. I could *emotionally accept them* either way.

The Science of Happiness

At last. After 50 years I'd found what I'd been hunting for—the foundation of a *science of happiness*. Now I had a clearer understanding of what I needed to do. It didn't mean I would have to stop doing the things I was doing. I could still enjoy sex and money or anything else I wanted as long as it was not harmful to others. I just had to eliminate the driving demands that distorted the integration of head and heart that produces wisdom. Paul, in the Bible, had expressed this when he wrote, "The love of money is the root of all evil." It wasn't money itself but the *love* of money—the addictive demand for money—that brought distorted value choices and unhappiness. My personal challenge was to notice

---

*PROGRAMMING: Learning, habits of mind, behavior patterns. Conscious or unconscious instructions installed in my mind that determine my feelings and guide my thoughts and actions. For example, "My programming is making me angry when I get caught in traffic," or "I have programming that enables me to feel patient in a traffic jam."

my addictive, robot-like demands—and turn them into preferences instead.

The good news was that I could be happy *even if I didn't get what I wanted!* I didn't have to beat my head bloody against the brick walls of reality. Suddenly it all made sense to me. I decided to devote the rest of my life to this inner work on myself. The road to happiness was clearer. I just had to follow it where it led me. I had reached a great turning point in my life!

11

My New Priorities

I had passed my 50th birthday. Several months earlier, I'd spent the Christmas week of 1970 with the lama. I was successfully operating a nationwide real estate company I had worked hard to create. I had started this company because I wanted financial security for the rest of my life.

New insights flooded into my mind. I realized that my desire for financial security is not necessarily connected with how many dollars I have: the more dollars, the more security. Instead it is relative: poverty is wanting more than I earn; richness is earning more than I want to spend. It occurred to me that I might voluntarily simplify my life: getting around in a van with a folding wheelchair ramp instead of a Cadillac with a strong attendant to lift me. Maybe I could live with a "family" of congenial friends who could help me physically.

Perhaps I could break out of a lifestyle dependent on financial success. I could work toward a simpler life with time to do the things I really liked, such as writing, teaching, taking care of my health, being close to nature, and spending more time with a life partner. What would happen if I set up a nonprofit organization, donated most of my money to it—and then trusted the universe to give me enough security, sensation, power, and love? It took me a year to develop this level of trust.

A New Lifestyle

After working hard learning how to play the money game, I resolved to make the break from my business and pleasure-oriented life. I wanted to explore the power of love that Christ had taught—with the non-attachment that Buddha had recommended. I wanted to spend the rest of my life learning how to love more and demand less. I decided to let go of my business.

I realized that an entirely new lifestyle would be difficult for my conservative father to understand. Several years earlier, he had told me that on his passing, about $600,000 would come to me as my inheritance. Although I'd worked hard to develop an independent security, I'd always felt that my father's wealth was my ace in the hole—that I would never be without money in my lifetime one way or another. And now I had to face the fact that my backup security through inheritance might not be there if he strongly disapproved of what I was doing.

I worked on my courage for months to be able to share my new direction with him. Finally, I went to his apartment overlooking Biscayne Bay in Miami. I had made up my mind to tell him everything about my plans that didn't meet his models. I had decided to leave my business. I was going to found a nonprofit organization and give my possessions to it. Next year I would be leaving for California in the Greyhound bus I'd recently bought and was remodeling into a motor home. It was a lot to throw at him. And it felt very freeing to straight-forwardly share my soap opera with him. Although I sat facing him, most of the time I avoided his silent sternness and looked instead at his wife, Polly, who listened to me with empathy. I had done it. I rolled out the door feeling tall.

My father had said very little to me that day. He was listening—not reacting. Several days later I got a letter from him. He felt sad that I was not "putting Jesus first" and he wanted me to "have faith in God." I've had to accept as one of life's ironies that his mind is so set in a fundamentalist framework that to him it is not enough that I devote my life to teaching love, which is an essence of Christ's guidance. He cannot accept my *experiencing* God and the infinite in my own way, instead of *believing* in his way. I honor the light that guides him. I deeply appreciate the way my life has been enriched by the many fine values and skills he has passed on to me. Today he is healthy and active—and over 90. May I do as well.

The Failure of My Success

I realized that I was past the half-century point in my life. I was without a life partner. I was heading into the elderly years when diseases sometimes begin to gnaw at the body. It didn't seem right. I had been a good boy and done everything that society said to do—I'd educated myself well, earned money, been married, had children, and achieved. On the outside I had lived a glamorous life—I was master of a large yacht, head of a thriving business, and author of several books, I had friends and lovers, and I enjoyed the prestige of a family name that was well recognized by the South Florida community. What more could I want? I had thought my life was great, and I had told myself I was happy. But the question had persisted, "Is this all there is? Is this IT?"

A small, quiet voice from my heart kept whispering softly, "There's more, Ken, there's more." I couldn't ignore it any longer. My heart longed for inner peace—and loving heart relationships with people. I had largely failed to achieve these things. My life looked great on the outside to all public appearances—I honestly did not know even one person with whom I would be willing to swap my life. And yet I began to realize that I was a failure inside in terms of the love in my heart, a lightness in the here and now, and a loving partner.

About two thousand years ago Paul had warned about the trap of outer success and inner failure. I'm sure I had read it in Sunday school; yet I had to "discover" it afresh from my own experience. I thought of the words he had so eloquently written:

> If I had the gift of being able to speak in other languages without learning them, and could speak in every language there is in all of heaven and earth, but didn't love others, I would only be making noise. If I had the gift of prophecy and knew all about what is going to happen in the future, knew everything about everything, but didn't love others, what good would it do? Even if I had the gift of faith so that I could speak to a mountain and make it move, I would still be worth nothing at all without love. If I gave everything I have to poor people, and if I were burned alive for preaching the Gospel but didn't love others, it would be of no value whatsoever.

Since I had not been attracted to the rigidity of my father's religion, a spiritual component had been largely lacking in my life. I'd been told that "God is love" but I couldn't hear it. I had been seeing things in terms of me vs. the world, and I had been trying to make sure I got my slice of the world's big pie. And now, although I did not know it at the time, I was on the verge of a spiritual awakening in which I would learn to bring the miraculous power of love into my life. I was discovering how to create the inner happiness that had previously been impossible no matter how hard I'd tried.

From Victim to Creative Cause

I could now spend my time unfolding what I would later call the "Science of Happiness." I wanted to formulate a teachable system that would encompass four parts: maintaining a healthy body; techniques for clear thinking; methods that would nurture love for oneself and others; and an awareness of the benefits of generosity in helping others.*

After turning my business over to an employee in the spring of 1971 (I did not want to hang around long enough to dispose of it to my advantage), I was ready for the next great gift that life had to offer me. The carrier of this wonderful gift was a woman named Jane.

I was living on the *Caprice* with about six people. There was no woman companion in my life when Jane arrived. She'd heard that there was a guy living on a yacht who was interested in meeting people. Her face was adorably framed by curly black hair. She had a lively manner and a good sense of humor. The people aboard liked her. When she seemed friendly toward me, I

---

* As the Science of Happiness developed, so did a conceptual framework and language to communicate about it. Since they became such an important part of my thinking, from now on in this book I will be using more of that language and referring often to the basic framework. Appendix 1 explains both and will help you better understand how I present the rest of my story.

invited her to move onto the boat—an invitation she accepted. Within a few days she moved into the cabin next to mine, and an intimacy famine of many months ended.

By now I understood that it was only my own demands that had deprived me of continuing my life with Bonita—who'd been perfect for me in so many ways. I had not been a victim of Bonita, or her jealousy or moodiness. I alone had been the cause of my experience with her. The outside "reality" had not done it to me; it was just my programmed *internal reaction* to the outside reality that had created my desire to get out of the marriage. I saw the pattern my programming had created in my life, and I was determined to break it.

As I moved toward a relationship with Jane, I decided that I would not leave this relationship *no matter what.* If our relationship did not last, it would be because Jane left—not I. I did not tell her of my resolve, but I made a mental pledge to myself that I would follow this personal guideline completely.

This decision had far-reaching consequences. I believe it enabled me to achieve a growth in the next six months that I probably would not have attained for the rest of my life. Unwaveringly following this pledge helped me work on my demands without bolting from the relationship—and blaming Jane as being impossible to live with.

Doing My Homework

One of the models I had for a woman who lived with me was that she would want to continuously relate to me. This meant that she should automatically sit near me when we ate and generally choose to be with me.

Jane on the bow of the *Caprice*, 1971

Although I had altered some of my old subject-object view of women, I still wanted her to be there for me sexually on a "reasonable" basis. I had the model that she always be honest with me. And I had the model that she understand and want to support me in the things I was doing in my life, and not be critical of me when she talked with other people—especially in a way that could undermine their cooperation.

In the next six months, I would learn that I had been holding these models as demands. Jane would give me the painful experiences I needed to change these demands into preferences.* She would violate almost every model I had for a happy relationship. She would provide the situations in which I would figuratively "smash my nerves raw" as she put me in touch with my demanding programs.

One of her first gifts was her choice not to sit next to me sometimes when we were eating. There were about six of us who would gather around a table in the salon. From the first evening, she began to rattle my model of how "my girlfriend" was supposed to act. Sometimes she would sit next to me and other times she wouldn't. It wasn't that she didn't sit next to me when we had some disagreement—there seemed to be no particular pattern. So instead of trying to change Jane, I began to work intensely on my internal programming to make it okay for Jane to sit anywhere she wanted at the table.

I kept reminding myself that it was my demand that was making me feel annoyed, not where Jane was

---

* PREFERENCE: A want or desire that does not trigger separating emotions or tensions in my body or mind whether or not it is satisfied. Using preferential programming, I can try to make changes, I can think I am right, but I emotionally accept what's happening. For example, "I prefer not to get caught in traffic, but I'm not making myself upset if I do."

sitting. I began to perceive my demand that she sit next to me as an attempt of my ego to continually prove that she was really my girlfriend—and make a public statement to others around us. So why couldn't she still be my girlfriend and sit four feet away from me at a table when we ate?

I tried to see my soap opera from a wider perspective. I noticed that my programming addictively demanded a certain arbitrary form so I could feel contented. I saw my reaction as involuntary, robot-like, as if I had no choice. "Let it go," I kept telling myself. Instead of changing Jane, *for the first time in my life, I wanted to let go of my demands*! After a few days of working on it, I found I had reprogrammed the demand into a preference.

Although I didn't see it that way at the time, I had learned my first lesson. I didn't know it, but this was only the beginning.

12

Jane's Gifts

I frequently enjoyed taking walks around the docks, seeing the various boats, and saying "hello" to people. Jane never wanted to stroll about in this way. I usually did not want to go alone. Again my models of how my girlfriend should act were not being met. But I had made a deep commitment to myself that I would use this relationship for my growth. If it ever dissolved, it would be at Jane's request—not mine. The next focus of my inner work was on creating a genuine emotional experience of *preferring* that we take occasional walks together—but not *demanding* it as a condition for letting myself feel happy.

Checking Out My Demanding Programming

After we had been together for a few weeks, it became clear that Jane wanted at times to be intimate with another man. She would go many days without being with me sexually. However, if I began expressing sexual energy toward another woman, she instantly felt jealous. I recalled how I had broken up with Bonita partly because she sometimes got "unreasonably" jealous. My life was now providing me with the gift of another experience that I labeled "unreasonable jealousy." I told myself that it was only fair—if Jane was relating to another man, I should be able to relate to another woman.

Again my commitment to growth came through for me. I told myself that if my ego could figure out a way to avoid working on its programming by judging another person wrong, it would do so. My ego also could have retreated from the situation by repressing, suppressing, or ignoring my resentment about her unreasonable jealousy. I knew that would have been the way to Ulcerville.

So I accepted the challenge to handle my separating feelings by reprogramming my addictive demand—by letting go of my demand that Jane not be jealous. I'd *prefer* that she not feel jealous if I paid attention to another woman, but I would not *demand* it as a condition of my remaining in the relationship. Jane's gifts were giving me a superb opportunity for dealing with my greatest hang-ups. My old programs had demanded that my girlfriend give me "enough" sex, and that she not be unreasonably jealous. And now a new light was guiding me.

I was no longer completely at the mercy of my ego's deception that my internal experience was determined by outside events. I was getting clearer and clearer about applying these noble truths in my life: (1) my life was definitely suffering, (2) my addictive demands (not outside events) were the cause of my suffering, and (3) the way to get rid of suffering was to get rid of my addictive demands—upleveling them to preferences instead.*

Night after night I lay alone in my bed wanting relief from the tyrannical grip of my demanding programming that Jane not sleep with someone else. I told myself that a few months earlier I did not even know Jane. Why should I now be so possessive and demanding of her? I found that my intellectual arguments and persuasive reasonings to myself did not relax the grip of my resentment, antagonism, anger, hurt, disappointment, and frustration. My emotions would not comply with the wishes of my intellect.

Day after day, the torture caused by my demands continued. Without repressing my feelings, I was determined to appreciate Jane for all that she gave me in my life—and not destroy my love and caring because of what she was not giving me. Jane was a bright, attractive, feminine energy in my life. When we had sex together, she was warm and loving; why couldn't I just appreciate what I did have—and let go of what I didn't have?

One's deeper levels of programming can be very tenacious. As I look back now, I realize that I had to have a relentless, determined woman like Jane who would not be swayed by compassion—or fear of rejection—to provide me with this great opportunity to stay in vivid touch with my demanding programming. I truly needed her for my growth.

---

* UPLEVEL: To change a demand into a preference. For example, "I upleveled my demand that I not get caught in traffic, although I still have a preference that I avoid traffic congestion."

Another Opportunity for Growth

As the summer continued, Jane would occasionally borrow small sums of money, like twenty-five to fifty dollars. She explained that her trust fund in New York was temporarily tied up and she would pay me back later. I introduced her to Jacque Fresco, my coauthor in *Looking Forward.* The three of us cooked up a dream of owning an entire island in the Bahamas on which we would begin in miniature to experience parts of the coming great new society as we conceived it—using 21st-century technology to support human values. Jane assured us that her trust fund would be available by the time we found the island.

We threw off the dock lines and headed across the gulf stream in the *Caprice.* We docked at Yachthaven in the colorful Nassau harbor. A real estate office there had several interesting possibilities to offer us. We traveled to some properties on the *Caprice,* and they arranged to show us more distant islands from a seaplane.

Transcendent Experiences

At this point of new direction, when I had just begun to consciously and intensely work to bring the power of love into my life, some unusual things happened inside me. While navigating through the Exuma Islands, I had an experience that transcended ordinary mental functioning. I felt an immense energy—a merging with the infinite. It felt like the pure energy of God—radiant, indescribable—and I felt a part of it all. It was not like my childhood image of an old man with a beard peering over a cloud, pulling the strings of the universe. It lasted a few minutes, and I tried to remain quiet afterwards to let it soak in. This was one of those benchmarks that have a subtle lifetime effect. It added to my changing perception of what life is all about.

Apparently my mind was open for more, because another experience happened during the same trip on the west coast of Eleuthera. I was sitting alone on the stern of the *Caprice* while we were under way. I was looking out the port side at the seemingly endless ocean. After several moments, I felt something new: *I was right here, right now.*

I had no flicker of thought about the past or future. The experience of the sights and sounds of "now" *expanded* to completely fill my entire awareness. Time stood still. It was deeply satisfying. Here and now was enough—even more than I needed to be happy. Although "nothing" was happening around me to interest or entertain me, my internal awareness of "being here now" was fully fulfilling! Life was expanding into new dimensions for me.

While searching for our Shangri-la in the form of a tropical island, I had found my own door to paradise inside me. I had awakened a little more. I would never fully return to my previous illusions. From now on, I would increasingly be *in* the world—but not *of* the world.

Jane's Deception

We returned to Miami after several weeks of looking for a location in the Bahamas. Then Jacque told me Jane was giving him a check for $100,000 for a down payment. My training with Alfred Korzybski had taught me to hold closely to factual experience and loosely to "verbal maps"—what people said. The mind is very adept in inventing a papier-mâché world of words and ideas. It can develop verbal ideas that have nothing to do with facts and realities in actual life situations. Korzybski emphasized what he called the natural order: facts first; then words. *Survey the territory* through observation; then formulate it into "verbal maps" that represent the nonverbal territory as adequately as possible.

Since my early twenties I had been mentally training myself in Korzybski's methods. Jane's allusions to her trust fund in New York existed for me only in the realm of "verbal mapping." As yet, I had observed no "nonverbal territory" to provide me with factual evidence of such a fund. Jane gave excuses why her funds were being delayed; I never saw correspondence from the trust company she said was administering the funds. I did not conclude that she did not have a trust fund. I simply kept an open mind on the subject for whichever way the map flopped. And I had been willing to play the game of life "as if" there really was a trust fund.

When I heard that Jane was about to give Jacque a large sum, I decided to begin checking out the territory. Jane had introduced me to a friend of hers named Russ. I called Russ and told him what was happening. He immediately said, "She's getting in trouble again." He told me that she had played the heiress game before and had gotten herself and others into some serious situations. I thanked him for this information and told him that he did not need to be concerned.

Now what to do? A suggestion from the separate-self department of my ego was to throw her out of my life.*

---

* SEPARATE-SELF: The illusory "me-vs.-them" perceptions that guard my security, sensation, and power demands. The mental programs that create the experience of life as a battle against myself, other people, and the world. For example, "My separate-self is mad about getting caught in the traffic jam, and I feel angry toward the other drivers."

She had been unfaithful to me, had lied to me, had brought me as much pain as pleasure, and was now involved in a con game. It was time to get out of the relationship.

My unified-self reminded me to use Jane's "gifts" for my own growth.* It reminded me of the commitment I'd made not to retreat from the relationship but instead to go forward lovingly into it—working on my demands. Clearly, my unified-self was gaining the upper hand in my thoughts, feelings, and motivations. From a mountaintop perspective, I could see Jane as a beautiful, young person who was doing her best to make her life work—although some of her programming was most unskillful and quite self-defeating in the long run.

I reminded myself that inner and outer honesty, understanding, compassion, patience, and heart-to-heart love were all I needed. Nothing could harm me except the demands of my separate-self ego. As long as my perception was generated by preferential programming, I could make my way through life safely and wisely.

Although my various loans to Jane totaled somewhere around $500, I had followed my own inner guideline of not loaning any money that I was not willing to transform into a gift should the circumstances warrant it. I had nothing at all to be concerned about. Life was simple—it was only my demands and expectations that make it seem so impossibly complex at times!

My next step was to call together the people who were part of the *Caprice* community at that time. We sat around in the salon on our pillows in the usual setting for

---

* UNIFIED-SELF: "Me-and-her" instead of "me-vs.-her" programming. Programming that gives me an overall perspective of how everything fits into my journey through life, either for my *growth* or for my *enjoyment.* My unified-self thus creates an experience of people and situations as a unified or integral part of my journey instead of a nuisance or threat. For example, "My unified-self patiently accepts the traffic jam."

our meetings. I couldn't tell if there was tension in the room, but I was clear that I wasn't there to blame Jane. With Jane present, I factually set forth the new information I had received from Russ. I did this without blaming Jane or trying to make her feel guilty for misleading us. I viewed her performance as one of life's gifts to check out the state of my own programming and to give me the opportunity to do inner work to develop more love in all the twistings and turnings of my life.

It could have been a sensational bombshell resulting in her righteous expulsion from our group—or her deciding to leave us when she was exposed. It turned out to be a bland session. I presented the facts so as to clear the air of illusions. None of us felt angry or righteous—Jane was just following the programming she happened to have at that time in her life. I was slowly learning to avoid the victim role. Instead I chose to be a creative cause of unconditional love within my own heart. And at the same time, I was truthful and realistic about everything. I was getting the hang of learning the lessons that life was offering me.

What I call the soap opera of material events in daily life always has a spiritual dimension—and vice versa. By insightfully using this life event as a message for my growth, I found myself integrating the material and the spiritual. It was good practice, because life was just getting me prepared for Jane's nuclear bomb.

13

My Triumph
Over Jealousy

Jane's greatest gift was still to come. Charles Berner, who operated the Institute of Ability at Lucerne Valley, California had held an "enlightenment intensive" in Coconut Grove about a year previously which I had attended. Jane became interested in taking a one-month training led by him at his California center. Since I had noticed from the beginning that Jane did not feel inner peace for very long at a time, I wanted her to benefit from this opportunity for growth. I told her I would furnish the funds for taking the seminar. She left in October 1971.

I wrote to her every day. In my occasional talk with her on the phone, I began to feel a subtle shift in her interest in me. I couldn't put my finger on anything that might be reduced to words. She reassured me that she would be coming back to Miami.

When the seminar was over, she called from California and said that Charles wanted to visit Miami. The words sounded fine—and I wondered what was really happening.

Assaulting My Programming

When they arrived, I was looking forward to spending the night with Jane after she'd been away for a month. When bedtime came Jane said to me, "I want to sleep with Charles tonight." Charles?! Well, here we go again, I told myself. I had dealt with this familiar tendency in Jane before, and apparently my programming would have to deal with it again.

Jane's stateroom was next to mine with only a plywood partition in between. I was astonished when I began to hear the unmistakable sounds of lovemaking. What about my feelings—how could they do this to me? The enthusiastic sounds of lovemaking that came through the thin partition were magnified by my ultra-attention. My separate-self triggered victim programming: "Unfair; not playing the game right; they are tormenting me with jealousy."

Nerve currents raced into the limbic area of my brain and generated intense emotions of jealousy, hurt, resentment, and frustration. Their prolonged lovemaking gradually increased in decibels. At the moment of climax, Charles shouted, "White light!" Without a doubt, Jane was giving me a superb opportunity for personal growth.

Never in my life have I experienced such jealousy; I couldn't sleep even after their lovemaking had subsided. My mind asked, "Why am I still clinging to demands that Jane meet my models of how 'my girlfriend' should treat me?" I worked on myself, doing my best to let go of these insistent addictive demands.

I call them "addictive" because an addiction is any-thing you tell yourself you *must have* to be happy. I clearly understood intellectually that my misery and suffering were being caused by my own demanding programming—not by Jane. It's true she was providing an outside stimulus, but it was the *programming* in my own *biocomputer* that was making me unhappy. Yet I couldn't let it go. I was really stuck. I finally called my attendant and asked him to take me down to the lower deck where others were sleeping. I woke them up and shared my feelings; they were understanding and in-sisted that I sleep in their room. About three in the morning I finally dropped off to sleep.

The next day Jane kept herself close to Charles. When I wanted to go out walking with her and talk with her alone, she politely declined. When I asked her if she wanted to be with Charles instead of me, she said, "I don't know."

Well, perhaps I still had a chance. I held back on expressing my strong feelings of resentment in order to appear cool on the surface throughout the next day. The "fair-unfair" department of my rational mind told me that it was only fair that tonight Jane would choose to sleep with me. I felt sure that after my being so understanding of her sleeping with Charles the first night, she would certainly be with me the next night. After all, why did she return to Miami? I wanted to talk with her alone and renew our relationship.

But she did not want to spend the next night with me. I just couldn't understand it. My hurt and jealousy became even more intense. I decided not to fight it. I moved to the lower deck and slept fitfully even though removed from the symphony of passion.

I Want to Be Free

The following day as I was taking a bath, I began to feel sorry for myself. I felt terribly trapped in my demanding program. I'd done everything I could to get free of it. And yet the intense stimulus of Jane and Charles's romance on the boat was too powerful for my programming to handle.

I had struggled for months with some success to get free of my demands that Jane meet my models for a partner. Since she and Charles had arrived two days before, I'd struggled in vain to get free in the far more intense situation they were providing me. I was trapped. I felt sorry for myself because I was a slave to my programming—an emotional slave. I'd lost my freedom to choose how my mind would respond in this situation.

I began to sob while sitting in the bathtub. Instead of directing animosity toward them, I focused on my own plight of being caught in the vise-grip of my demanding programmings. I began to cry and to say over and over to myself, "I want to be free, I want to be free."

This referred to my freedom from the possessive programming that made me trigger jealousy; *it did not refer to freedom from the relationship with Jane.* It was more important for me to be free of my demanding programming (and the suffering it caused me) than for Jane to be different. I wanted the freedom from pain that only my own inner growth could give me—not the temporary freedom I could have by retreating from this situation that was triggering my demands. I said to myself over and over, "I want to love Jane and Charles." I still hoped she would choose to be with me—but I would not willfully try to force any particular pattern of relationship on her.

I discovered that the phrase "It's okay for Jane to love Charles" gradually lost its ability to keep me sobbing. I switched to another phrase, "I can get free from my clinging." I continued saying these reprogramming phrases over and over—sobbing intensely yet quietly. I somehow knew that I had to keep going *until the phrases had lost their emotional potency to trigger my crying.* By saying these and similar phrases intensely, I would burn out the demands that were triggering my jealousy.

Had reprogramming occurred? To test it, about ten minutes after switching phrases I would go back to a previous one to see if it had really lost its sting. Sometimes no cloudy feelings developed; with other phrases a few hundred more repetitions would be needed.

I was constantly searching for phrases that made me sob most intensely. I used each phrase until there was no more emotional response. Part of me was suffering from the tyranny of my clinging programming; there was also a part of me that was busy directing this and enjoying it all.

Finally I had worn out all of the phrases; none of these or any others I tried could keep me crying. I realized that whatever it was, the process was finished.

Throughout the entire experience of an hour and a half, I had a mountaintop perspective that I was doing something very important. I felt my growth was tied in with the repetition that deeply implanted these new phrases, which expressed the way I *wanted* my programming to work.

I later concluded that whatever I tell myself (either positive or negative) when I have strong emotions will be deeply etched on my mind. Today I'd sooner pet a

Jane and Charles in Miami, 1971

rattlesnake than poison my perception by repeating negative, judgmental thoughts in my mind.

Was I Really Free?

It had stopped itself. What had I done? I had treated my clinging programming as "the enemy." I had not blamed others—or myself—for my unhappiness. I had used my emotions to track down the phrases that triggered the strongest feelings of jealousy. I had found positive statements that expressed new instructions to my biocomputer, such as "I want to accept Jane and Charles as they are." I had tensed my body, built up the emotional voltage, and cried as I *consciously* used these reprogramming phrases to burn out the undesired programs that triggered jealousy—and install the programs I wanted in my mind. I had avoided calming down as long as I could find a phrase that had emotional juice for me.

I felt both very drained and extremely high. I had a feeling that nothing could adversely affect me—that I had a oneness with everything in my life. I wondered whether this experience would continue when I saw Jane and Charles together.

I got dressed and went up to the front of the boat. He was sitting on a stool and she was affectionately leaning against him. I felt only love for both of them—not even a twinge of jealousy. It had worked! I felt that I was through with jealousy for the rest of my life! I had reprogrammed the demands that created my jealousy. And I had done this without either *suppressing* or *expressing* hostile, separating feelings. By being in touch with my feelings and using them as a catalyst, I had rid myself of undesired programming. Reprogramming really worked! If I applied myself, I *could* be the master of my emotions.

Three Ways to Handle Jealousy

It took me a little while to realize the significance of this experience. I had stumbled on a technique that enabled me to bridge the gap between what my intellect wanted and what my emotions felt—for integrating the right and left brain! I had found a way to truly change my emotions without suppressing them.

I realized there were three ways I could have dealt with the jealousy. I saw that I could have stuffed down and *suppressed* the jealousy and hurt—but the feelings really wouldn't have gone away. The smothered emotions bumping around in my subconscious mind could have caused psychosomatic problems.

Or I could have lashed out at Jane or Charles—and felt better for having *expressed* my hostility and gotten it off my chest. This would have insured that I wasn't suppressing. But the same feelings would have kept coming up every time something like this happened. I didn't want to live through more of that agony.

I became aware that what I had done was to go straight to the source of the jealousy and hurt—the demanding programming. I had worked to *reprogram* the demands that *caused* the jealousy. They just would not arise in the future. I had removed the *cause*—not just dealt with the *effects*.

Working to get rid of the demand was very different from smothering the emotional symptoms. I hadn't reprogrammed my feelings of jealousy. I had reprogrammed the demand that had caused them. I had used jealousy as a guide dog to find my demand and to test my progress in reprogramming.*

I had received an intense experience I had needed to get free of jealousy for a lifetime. What an incredible gift! I decided to call this technique "Consciousness Focusing." It became one of the Living Love methods that I began to teach when I founded my school about a year later.

The next day I asked both Jane and Charles whether they wanted to continue their relationship—or if Jane wanted to be with me in Miami. They chose to leave together. I had chosen to give myself a great lesson in personal growth that would add to my happiness for the rest of my life.

The Message of the Sunset

It was time for a cruise in the Bahamas. About 12 of us went to Highburn Key in the Exuma group of islands. I had no partner on this trip—and I felt lonely and deprived. I had done so much work on my addictive programming about sex and relationships, yet I still had more inner work to do. I was with friends in an idyllic setting but, like the Garden of Eden, my programming was making me unhappy because I did not have the apple of my eye.

In the late afternoon, I got on the dock and went up a hill alone in my motorized chair. From the highest

*This technique is explained in Chapter 9 of *Gathering Power Through Insight and Love* and Chapters 14 and 15 of *Handbook to Higher Consciousness*. It is also described in an audiotape, "My Triumph Over Jealousy," recorded soon after the technique was discovered. These are available through the Ken Keyes College Bookroom, 790 Commercial Avenue, Coos Bay, OR 97420.

point on the island I had a panoramic view. The sky was a radiant yellow. As I watched the sun setting into the water, I moved into experiencing my loneliness as caused by my demands—and I began to let go. I relaxed and felt totally in the moment—no thoughts of "wouldn't it be wonderful if I had a partner." Life was enough. I was enough!

I just sat there enjoying it all for about 45 minutes! I felt that from that time on, I would no longer *demand* a life companion. I could enjoy my life whether I had one or not—even though I knew I would always strongly *prefer* to have a partner if the universe provided one. Another step toward freedom. It was getting dark and I returned to the *Caprice*. The ambience of the boat had changed for me—it was now a more satisfying place.

I knew that I was on the path to creating my life at higher levels of happiness and fulfillment. During this trip, I completed the Twelve Pathways. They became, to me, a condensation of philosophical, psychological, and spiritual wisdom from the ages. I boiled the ideas down to simple affirmations that I and others could instantly use. Knowing something is only the first step. The benefits come when we use the knowledge in the heat of the moment when we need it. Once formulated, I could use these little gems for guidance and reminders whenever I felt frustration, hurt, or anger.

I wanted to tell people everything I was doing that was making such a remarkable difference for me. Even if I chewed their ears off for a half hour, I couldn't get it all in. I decided to write it down for people to read if they were interested. Dictating rapidly, it was done in a month. I titled it *Living Love—A Way to Higher Consciousness*.

The Twelve Pathways
To Unconditional Love and Happiness

Freeing Myself

1. I am freeing myself from security, sensation, and power addictions that make me try to forcefully control situations in my life, and thus destroy my serenity and keep me from loving myself and others.

2. I am discovering how my consciousness-dominating addictions create my illusory version of the changing world of people and situations around me.

3. I welcome the opportunity (even if painful) that my minute-to-minute experience offers me to become aware of the addictions I must reprogram to be liberated from my robot-like emotional patterns.

Being Here Now

4. I always remember that I have everything I need to enjoy my here and now—unless I am letting my consciousness be dominated by demands and expectations based on the dead past or the imagined future.

5. I take full responsibility here and now for everything I experience, for it is my own programming that creates my actions and also influences the reactions of people around me.

6. I accept myself completely here and now and consciously experience everything I feel, think, say, and do (including my emotion-backed addictions) as a necessary part of my growth into higher consciousness.

Interacting With Others

7. I open myself genuinely to all people by being willing to fully communicate my deepest feelings, since hiding in any degree keeps me stuck in my illusion of separateness from other people.

8. I feel with loving compassion the problems of others without getting caught up emotionally in their predicaments that are offering them messages they need for their growth.

9. I act freely when I am tuned-in, centered, and loving, but if possible I avoid acting when I am emotionally upset and depriving myself of the wisdom that flows from love and expanded consciousness.

Discovering My Conscious-Awareness

10. I am continually calming the restless scanning of my rational mind in order to perceive the finer energies that enable me to unitively merge with everything around me.

11. I am constantly aware of which of the Seven Centers of Consciousness I am using, and I feel my energy, perceptiveness, love, and inner peace growing as I open all of the Centers of Consciousness.

12. I am perceiving everyone, including myself, as an awakening being who is here to claim his or her birthright to the higher consciousness planes of unconditional love and oneness.

The popular confusion between love and sex made me ponder about calling my personal growth system "Living Love." I suspected that some people would read that as "Living Sex." But what alternative was there? "Living Agape"? No one would buy that.

I had 1,000 copies printed locally that I could give to people when I talked with them. To my surprise, I started getting orders in the mail. Some people were using the Pathways in the book for guidance, memorizing them and saying them as reprogramming phrases. Over the next few years, I greatly enlarged and retitled it *Handbook to Higher Consciousness*. I didn't advertise. Bookstores started stocking it. People often bought a half dozen copies for their friends. I never dreamed that this book would one day become a bestseller. Now 18 years later, it is still selling steadily and over a million copies have been printed.

14

Discovering My On-Off Sex Switch

My next step was to finish remodeling the ex-Greyhound bus. I worked out a way to build my turnover bed in the back. After installing it, I changed my mind. I had it taken out. This would help to unclutter my life. Similarly a lifetime of accumulated books, furnishings, clothes, and other stuff of mine enriched people at the marina—or the Miami dump. It felt good preparing to travel light. Possessions can clutter your life so much that they own you instead of you owning them. I wanted to shake loose my materialistic roots in Miami and leave behind a life motivated by profit and pleasure. I sold the *Caprice* at a bargain price of $15,000.

For the first time in about a quarter century I was without professional attendants. Although medically classified as completely disabled, I was ready to trust the universe through the power of love to give me everything I needed.

One of the changes I noticed as I moved into an inner space of peace and relaxation involved urinating. Before I found Living Love, I had a frequency and urgency problem. Sometimes when I was unable to get to a bathroom, I would wet my pants. To avoid this, I always kept a portable urinal near me. Once Living Love became a part of my approach to life, the urgency greatly diminished. It's amazing to me that on a 17-hour flight from Los Angeles to Sydney, Australia, I had no urgency and comfortably retained up to a quart.

In June 1972 I left Miami with friends who wished to join me in an alternative style of life. I wasn't just leaving a city I had known and loved since age four. I was setting out for a life of contribution and service. I didn't know where I would end up or what I would do. I thought we might find a farm somewhere that I could open up to people with whom I might share the Science of Happiness. I was in no hurry to get anywhere special. I wanted to meet more like-minded people and keep learning and growing. I had said good-bye to my father and Clara Lu. Kenny was away. Twee went with us to Disney World near Orlando. We spent a day enjoying rides and shows together. Then she took a bus back to Miami, and we headed for the Rainbow Gathering in the Rocky Mountain National Park in Colorado.

The Aquarian Ark

About this time we christened the motor home the *Aquarian Ark.* We spent a month in the Taos, New Mexico area, visiting the Lama Foundation on Sundays. Each morning I held a session for the people on the bus in which they used the Living Love processes I was putting together. The processes were designed to help folks find skillful ways to sort out their differences, and to stop "stashing" or hiding their separating emotions. They helped people take responsibility for their feelings and deal directly with the programming that caused the emotions. Realizing that the teaching methodology was becoming more and more effective, I decided I wanted to set up a teaching center. It seemed that California would be ideal. Eventually we arrived in California, and I began looking for a suitable building. I had a street artist paint "Living Love—A Way to Higher Consciousness" on both sides of the bus in letters about eight inches high.

I lived aboard the motor home for about a year after leaving Miami. In many ways it was like living on the boat—the bedroom, bathroom, kitchen, storage areas, and living room were all much smaller than in a home. I met people and invited them to travel with us. Some stayed a short time and some remained for months. We parked at the houses of friends or at motor home parks or found our own campsite in the woods.

Soon after my arrival in California, the people with me began to leave one by one. Finally there was just one man, Gil, and myself on the bus. Gil wanted to leave as soon as possible. Since I depended on other people to give me life support, this could have been a panic situation for me—it certainly would have been in the past. Somehow my trust enabled me to meet this predicament without any concern or alarm.

We had recently come to Berkeley from San Diego and were parked overnight on the side of a street. The next morning we started up the bus and began to pull away. Suddenly we heard a pounding on the bus and yelling from the curb side. We stopped, and a young man came aboard. He introduced himself as Bill and said he had been at Marion Petty's farm in Virginia. I had mailed Marion several dozen copies of *Living Love—A Way to Higher Consciousness* soon after it was printed in Miami. Marion had given Bill a copy. Bill had noticed the lettering on the side of the bus the previous night after we had parked the bus and gone to sleep. He had stayed awake all night at the gas station across the street, watching for signs of activity inside the bus.

Gil left within hours. Bill was the mainstay of my support at the first training I gave later that year, and for several years after we opened the Living Love Center in Berkeley.

Being Here Now

As I began doing trainings aboard the bus, more and more people became interested in becoming a part of our staff. One day, several of us were traveling in the motor home near the foothills of the Sierras in California. A woman had recently come aboard to join us. We had a "family-type" lifestyle in which occasional nudity when changing clothes was an accepted behavior. Nudity like this is not a sexually stimulating experience—it soon becomes ho-hum. Nevertheless, it occurred to me that I had not seen her without clothes since she'd been aboard. We pulled up near a stream, and everyone except myself got out to take a skinny dip. The stream was about 200 feet away, and I was sitting up front in the motor home, watching the folks go into the water. The new lady was just about to pull off her dress when there was a knock at the door of the motor home.

I turned and saw a man from a van parked nearby. He asked if I had a container he could put some oil in. I told him to come aboard, and we went back to the kitchen area. I found a jar we didn't need. He left, and I stayed toward the rear near the kitchen cabinet. After

30 seconds it occurred to me that I'd been about to see the new lady slip out of her clothes. I went up front, but her body was now hidden in the stream.

Then it dawned on me that I had passed a milestone in my addiction to sex. Someone had knocked on the door asking for a container. In the past my mind would have impatiently rejected this as a resented interruption of something that it wanted to do: relish the new woman disrobing.

But it had not happened that way. With no resistance, my attention had instead totally and naturally turned toward the visitor. I'd completely dropped the previous chain of perception for the moment. I had gone to the back of the motor home to serve the stranger's needs. After he'd left, my mind had not instantly sprung into "At last he's gone—now I get to look again." Instead, about a half minute had passed before my attention had returned to thinking about the disrobing lady.

Wow! Sex was becoming a more balanced activity in my mind instead of a dominating, overriding program that undermined many other values in my life. Small as it was, this was the first really tangible proof that I was breaking loose from sexual addiction. The old programming that had tenaciously operated for so many years was gradually being replaced with nondemanding patterns of thought that I now wanted. I was encouraged and inspired!

Mastering Sensation Demands

A few months later I was living aboard the motor home in Berkeley. It had been several months since I had experienced sex. An attractive woman named Cookie had accepted my invitation to be together and have sex that night. The next morning when we woke up, I wanted to repeat the mutual delights of the previous evening. She was not interested. "Give her time," I told myself. I put my arm around her, and we just lay there and talked. Any attempt to intimately touch her was quickly met by, "I don't want to do anything this morning." I kept patiently and gently pushing—and she patiently and gently said no.

I couldn't even tell myself I was needy—just greedy. And then it hit me. The universe had given me a beautiful experience the previous evening, but my programmed expectations and demands were insistently wanting more. I was plodding along the subtle edge of alienation that sexual pushiness creates. What a stupid behavior on my part—especially considering the satisfaction the night before.

I told myself, "I wish there were a switch in my brain that would let me cut off sexual desire when it isn't in the flow of the here and now." I imagined there was such a switch. I reached up and flicked it with an imaginary finger. It worked! When I flipped that imaginary sexual desire switch in my mind, my sexual energy immediately drained away. It was almost like turning out a light bulb!

How nice it was to be able to lie there with her, warmly communicating, and feeling close. I was free of the sexual compulsiveness that created separateness when I wanted it and she didn't. Could I be the master of my sexual desires? Was it that simple? Could it be that some elements of wisdom in the area of sex were beginning to take root? I wondered if this switch would work at other times. I found that it would. From then on, whenever I needed it, I could flick that imaginary, sexual desire switch—and cool it. The experience with Cookie had given me a valuable gift.

I don't know whether the mental sex switch technique will work for other people. Perhaps each of us needs to find our own ways to most effectively create the programming we want in our lives. One thing I'm sure of: demanding tapes don't have to be as disrupting of relationships as I made them for so many years. I know I can uplevel them to preferences if I really want to.

Easily Letting Go

That December I visited Esalen and asked if I could put up an announcement offering a one-week workshop on the Living Love techniques. They let me put up a notice on the bulletin board and gave me a meeting room where I could tell people about the workshop. About eight signed up. Several days later we traveled to a motor home park on the beach in Santa Cruz, and I gave my first Living Love workshop. I liked helping people learn about Living Love.

In January 1973 I rented a driveway in Berkeley, California, parked in it, and began doing weekend trainings on the motor home with up to six participants. In April I found the place I'd been looking for. It was an ex-fraternity house north of the Berkeley University of California campus. It had four stories, many rooms, and a sunken garden with Strawberry Creek running through it. In June the Living Love Center in Berkeley was opened. I began leading weekend personal growth workshops on a regular monthly schedule that by November had as many as 50 participants. Within a year, I was doing workshops in Los Angeles every three months, using the motor home to transport the teams of about eight people that supported the workshops. The *Handbook to Higher Consciousness* began to sell over fifty

The Living Love Center
in Berkeley, California, 1975

thousand copies a year, and our trainings attracted people from all over the United States.

Freedom from the grip of my sexual programming was at last happening for me. There was a third milestone, which assured me of the inner progress I had made. I was in a relationship with Karen. We had just returned home after spending an evening together having dinner in San Francisco's Chinatown. We were in the midst of having sex before going to sleep. Then she said, "I've got a headache. I'm really not into it." I instantly responded by saying, "That's okay. Let's snuggle up and go to sleep."

As I heard these words come from my mouth, I could hardly believe it. In the past, my programming would have answered, "Hold on just a few more seconds," or "You don't want to leave me this way, do you?" But these thoughts did not flash by my mind until I was analyzing the incident later. I had broken out of the jail of my sexually demanding programming.

I deeply value political freedom and "liberty and justice for all." I also consider *internal* freedom from demanding habits of mind as even more important for my happiness. To me, it's the greater freedom and it unfortunately can't be guaranteed by the Bill of Rights. However, it's a freedom we can all give ourselves.

Appreciating Monogamy

The liberation I felt as I escaped from my sexually demanding programming enabled me to gradually work toward another insight. I began to tell myself that most women in our culture have a deep level of programming (both conscious and unconscious) that favors a monogamous relationship. Even if a woman goes along with her partner's relating sexually to other women, she is likely to begin investing time in an outside relationship: "I'll get even with him," or "If it's okay for him, it's okay for me." If she remains monogamous, she may diminish her deeper levels of togetherness and love.

I had already grown past the dichotomy of shoulds and shouldn'ts in my life. Whether to have sex or not was a practical matter of what was best—both for me and a partner. Would it add unity—or separateness? After years of trying to make sexual plurality work in my life, I concluded that my search for togetherness would be more satisfying *to me* with monogamy. My inner wisdom began to view sexual fidelity as a *needed component* in creating the richness of "oneness" with a life partner.

And so my life took another giant flip-flop. This change helped me get on with my growth, for I could now explore the power of heart-to-heart love in greater depth. I was no longer jeopardizing the loving energy between my partner and myself by trying to combine a deeply loving relationship with occasional sexual variety. From now on, monogamy was the way to go for me—not as a matter of outer-imposed moral codes, but from an inner understanding that a deeper and deeper heart bond with one partner could be more satisfying for me.

I have observed that for most couples an occasional hit of sexual variety carries a big price tag. The antagonism, jealousy, decreasing trust, and instability of sexually open relationships usually create a bumpy way to run one's life. For the past 12 years of my life, I have been monogamous—completely faithful to my partner. I found it really works to give me the level of love and togetherness that I know today is much more satisfying.

And now that incurable herpes and lethal AIDS further complicate things, I appreciate even more my decision that led me to monogamy in the mid-seventies.

Graduating From Sexual Addiction

I no longer feel driven by sexual desires—and I do appreciate sex when it is a simple gift of a loving life together with my partner. Instead of trying to use sex as a major source of pleasure in my life, I now experience it as a delightful game to be enjoyed when it mutually happens. Instead of experiencing disappointment when sex doesn't happen the way I want it when I want it, I feel totally invulnerable today to any experience of disappointment, irritation, or frustration whether sex happens or not. Sexual energy today *can only add* to my enjoyment of life—since I've reprogrammed my demanding models of how it "should" be. I can just enjoy what is—or what isn't!

One benefit of evolving beyond my insistent desires for sex is that women today will often choose to be openly affectionate and to hug me, since their intuition tells them that I'm not looking for a sexual relationship. I'm no longer a possible threat. They feel that their warmth and closeness will not be misinterpreted by me as a come-on signal. Women don't like to open their hearts in a loving, affectionate way to a man, and then be accused of giving mixed messages. I've learned to give body language signals that I just want heart-to-heart love. This lets me create and inhabit a world in which I get to hug and enjoy a warm friendship with almost everyone—both men and women.

I feel that I have given myself the great gift of graduating from the never-ending craving for sensations because I have been fortunate enough to learn most of the sensation lessons. This progress helped me to go beyond being controlled by genital itches.

We all must start our journey from where we are— not from where we wish we were. My pride/prestige programming would love to downplay my past preoccupation with sensation, and instead talk about my great search for "the meaning of life," "God and the Infinite," or "how best to serve the world." But a much stronger part of my programming has chosen to be honest about what happened rather than suppress or idealize my story to make me look good.

I want to share my living truth by being forthright with where I have been hung up. I feel that a big part of my message is to show *how I used my unskillful programs* to eventually go beyond sensation compulsions, bring the power of love into my life, tune-in to the Infinite, and find a deep satisfaction in loving and serving the world. I think that no matter what the limiting personal programs happen to be for each of us, if we face them squarely we can grow out of them.

Security, sensation, power, and love. Personal growth takes patience and time. It felt good to be on my way, I hoped, to deeper levels of heart-to-heart love.

15

The Fruits of Cornucopia

When I first opened the Living Love Center, I recruited my staff from people off the street in Berkeley who seemed most open to expanding the frontiers of the spirit. All were volunteers; the staff received room, food, and $50 per month. Community spirit was high; service to others inspired us.

Many of these people in 1973 were involved in psychedelics. I would point out that to get the benefits of the Living Love methods, they would have to use the techniques when they were upset—not just relax by lighting up a joint. People who developed skill in using the methods, instead of continuing to use drugs, got the most benefits. Beginning in 1974, anyone who used an illegal substance on the property was asked to leave.

The books started selling rapidly. One of our trainers, Tolly Burkan, and I wrote *How to Make Your Life Work or Why Aren't You Happy?*—now titled *Your Life*

Is a Gift. (Tolly later authored *Dying to Live* and *Guiding Yourself Into a Spiritual Reality.*) I retitled my book on thinking *Taming Your Mind,* and renamed my nutrition book *Loving Your Body.*

Among the people who joined our staff was a Hollywood actress, Colin Wilcox-Horne, who had starred in *To Kill a Mockingbird* with Gregory Peck. She helped us organize the recording of our first album of Living Love songs. Marcus Allen, who later became a successful publisher, wrote and performed in our first two albums. Summer Raven wrote many Living Love songs, including my favorite, "I Just Go On Loving You," which was included in our first album. Shakti Gawain, who later wrote the popular *Creative Visualization* and *Living In the Light,* was on our staff for over a year. The Living Love Center was electrified by the energy of heart-to-heart love.

The weekend workshop that effectively presented the Living Love methods continued to be polished by my coleader, Kris Nevius, and myself. I usually rented a conference room in a major hotel for workshops outside our Berkeley headquarters. The atmosphere of a drab space became dramatically transformed into what felt like a Living Love workshop room. Posters and banners with messages such as "Love everyone unconditionally—including yourself" adorned the walls. We tried to make the workshops entertaining and at the same time offer people practical methods they could use to add to their happiness for the rest of their lives. These workshops were very successful, and our reputation spread quickly by word of mouth. In the larger cities, there were frequently over 100 participants.

Love in Action

Twee came out to visit me at Christmas in 1974 and even took our first week-long Joy of Living training. Later my son Kenny took a one-month training. As I developed my skill in *living love*, I wanted to work toward creating more understanding and love with Roberta, my children, and my father. I put them on the mailing list to receive our quarterly catalog so they would have more information about me. I enhanced my remembrances on their birthdays and at Christmas. I made a point of scheduling a yearly workshop in Miami so that I could visit my family. Gradually and imperceptibly over a period of years, more warmth came into my relationships with my father and Clara Lu.

I remember visiting Lu, her husband Bob, and my grandson Casey one summer evening around 1976. When it was the usual time to go, I found that I did not want to leave—and I had the feeling that Lu did not want me to leave either. It had worked!

The understanding and affection that developed between us has continued to increase. She and my wife, Penny, have now become good friends—and although she's ten years older than Penny, she has repeatedly told us she's glad we're together. I again had more evidence that when we open our hearts with unconditional love, our love will usually be mirrored back to us.

Setting Up the Lesson

A dynamic woman named Carole joined our staff in 1976. She had operated a small personal growth center in her home in Phoenix, Arizona. I first met her the previous year when she sponsored a weekend workshop I led in Phoenix. When Carole came to the Living Love Center in Berkeley, she rapidly absorbed the Living Love system and had strong rapport with other staff members. She was highly qualified, both administratively and in her ability to supervise successful trainings. The center needed a new Training Director and I put her in charge. Since she was so capable, I didn't think I needed to supervise her closely.

After a few months I was told that Carole's attitude was subtly influencing the staff. I was also noticing a shift in the cooperativeness of people supporting me in the workshops I was leading. I told Carole I would like to attend some of her staff meetings, and she replied that my presence would be confusing to the staff. And so I found myself in a dilemma. Here was a take-charge person, excellent at both leading trainings and administration, who seemed to be building a base of support in a separating me-vs.-Ken manner instead of an inclusive me-and-Ken attitude. What to do?

I ended up having a frank talk with Carole and telling her about my concerns. I asked her for her cooperation in supporting me in my role as leader of the growing Living Love organization. I told Carole that if we considered my effectiveness as one unit, and her effectiveness as one unit, and if we worked together, we could have the effectiveness of *ten* units in helping people with Living Love trainings.

Carole seemed to understand what I was talking about. She said that she would be glad to work with me in this way. I felt we had solved our differences.

By 1977, we'd outgrown the Living Love Center opened four years previously. We had about 30,000 people on our mailing list. We put the word out to them through our catalog that we were looking for a bigger place. Someone in Kentucky told us about a beautiful 150-acre college in St. Mary that had a century-old tradition as a Catholic seminary. Carole, Tony Cantea (our administrator), my lady friend Romi, and I flew out to see it. It was magnificently tucked into the rolling Kentucky hills with stately trees and excellent accommodations for several hundred students and staff. Because of its expansiveness, operating it would be a big job. I would not have bid for it if Carole hadn't assured me that she was willing to shoulder much of the responsibility. I saw the potential of what it could offer people and I welcomed her energy to make it work.

As it turned out, there were four bidders for the property and ours was next to the lowest. Because the Catholic Fathers felt that we were more compatible with the property's spiritual tradition, we won the bid. We purchased the property in July 1977, and because of its beauty and abundant provisions, we named it Cornucopia. We sold the Berkeley center to a student cooperative at a bargain price that was interest-free for five years. In August we left the Living Love Center and moved to Cornucopia. Less than a year after Carole had become Training Director, I also appointed her as the head administrator of Cornucopia.

My Conflict With Carole

Soon after we moved to our new headquarters in St. Mary, it became clear that Carole was not working with me as I had asked. One of the first issues that came up had to do with the team that had supported me when I led weekend workshops with Kris throughout the nation. Kris and I had worked together over four years

The Cornucopia
Institute at St. Mary,
Kentucky, 1977

Carole leading a class
at Cornucopia, 1978

developing a most effective weekend workshop. I wanted a specialized team that the two of us had personally trained that would work in a coordinated way to give the best workshops possible for teaching the power of love.

Carole did not want to furnish a permanent team of people to work with me. Instead she wanted to give me helpers for two or three workshops at a time and then replace them. She was concerned that the staff might develop ego territoriality, and she did not want any of them getting into an "I'm on Ken's workshop team" mind-set. I explained that I couldn't continually train people in that short time to give the high-quality workshops I felt good about. She was firm in her unwillingness to support me in the way I felt I needed to continue the high energy workshops I had been doing twice a month since 1972. Since quality was vital to me, I stopped doing nationwide trainings.

She did not want me leading trainings at Cornucopia except for the weekend workshop with Kris, nor did she want me to design new trainings for other trainers to give. The only job Carole wanted me to have at Cornucopia was to take responsibility for the cash flow and make financial decisions. I told her I didn't want to do this. I had spent most of my business life managing money, and now my enthusiasm was for doing trainings and guiding our new institute on a policy level.

I interpreted Carole's stand as meaning that she felt she had successfully created a personal empire that she wanted to run by herself. I told myself that my presence at Cornucopia would imply that I was tacitly approving of all that was happening—and I didn't. Since Carole did not wish to include me in decision-making, my power/ pride programming told me to move back to California to continue my writing and teaching. Thus, the universe set up an interesting power conflict for my programming to deal with. I dealt with this situation by withdrawing.

My programming justified this retreat by saying all I really wanted was to have a strong training institute that would teach the Living Love techniques for increasing happiness. Carole had great abilities and the loyalty of the staff, and she obviously chose to take full responsibility without any help from me. I would stay out of her way, let her do the job, and hope it all worked out for the best.

It was a difficult and challenging decision for me. I felt disappointed over not being more involved. But, I told myself, the main thing was to get the job done to benefit the students. What difference did it make who ran Cornucopia?

I thought at the time that I was skillfully avoiding a me-vs.-Carole power confrontation in which things could wind up so tightly that there would be no winner. I was wrong. As I look back today, I tell myself that I was operating from old programming that wanted everyone to get along. And so I avoided this crucial issue by retreating—and thus I left Carole to live with the results of her decisions.

In March 1978, I headed out with six people to set up another training center a half continent away. About a third of the people on our mailing list were in California. I thought two centers in the U.S. could offer more service than one. In the summer of 1978, I moved into a small apartment on Mission Drive in Santa Cruz, California. I lived with several people who studied with me, ran the household, took care of me physically, and helped me look at properties for a West Coast center.

Clouds Over Cornucopia

Carole and I both wanted Cornucopia to fulfill its destiny. When I moved away, I told Carole that I would leave the administration in her hands as long as she did two things: teach Living Love and pay the bills. As I see it, she met both of these requirements as long as we had the momentum from the Berkeley Living Love Center. Unfortunately, the academic and personal development standards for trainers became uneven in quality. In several workshops in other cities, some trainers were so unskillful that many people left the trainings early. The focus of Cornucopia gradually shifted toward building a community, which diminished the training energy. Several students at Cornucopia told me they had the feeling that they were intruding in someone's home. Some of our best trainers lost interest in leading workshops. Enrollments dropped. Eventually there was an accumulation of $45,000 in unpaid bills.

Looking back, I can see how I failed to respond sufficiently to the early signals Carole gave me in Berkeley. My overeagerness to reach more people through my life work threw my wisdom out of balance. I recognize now that I have had a pattern of delegating authority too rapidly without properly supervising.

If I could have done it over, I would have been willing to confront Carole and to insist on her accepting my supervision. I would not have been so addicted to everything running smoothly and harmoniously between us. I would have avoided a me-vs.-Carole feeling and kept a me-and-Carole perspective. I would not have avoided confrontations, hoping that all would work out for the best. I would have been willing to communicate back and forth with more patience and understanding to find win-win solutions. I would have worked on my power/pride programming that demanded that Carole want to follow my leadership—or I'd pick up my marbles and leave.

Carole was intuitive and brilliant in her teaching. She helped people to feel loved. She created a deep level of loyalty with her staff by individually and personally relating to and caring for each person—knowing what they wanted and often helping them get it. I think my business experience and dedication to helping people use the methodology that had come together for me had allowed the Berkeley center to flourish. My on-the-road trainings and books were an effective outreach for bringing people to the center. In combination, our strengths would have made a terrific leadership team if we had only had the skill to work out our conflicts.

I don't blame myself or Carole for how things turned out. This was a tough lesson for me. I hope I've learned it. And I honor the growth that took place during the five years of Cornucopia. Thousands of individuals experienced positive and unforgettable changes in their lives, and were touched with the beauty of love that was shared in a setting of creativity and acceptance. In spite of it all, I love Carole and appreciate all the good she did, and I am grateful for the fruits that Cornucopia gave to so many.

Part IV
Finding the Love
in My Heart

16

My Illusions About Love

I was now embarked on a new phase in my life. Since I was detached from the regular schedule of trainings I'd done for years, the busyness had gone out of my life. I had more time for reflecting, more inner and outer peacefulness to gain new perspectives on the matter of loving.

I had studied psychology in college. I noticed that many texts in psychology didn't even list "love" in their index. I had learned that the Greek word *agape* refers to unconditional love. Yet Webster's Ninth New Collegiate Dictionary offers two unenlightening definitions for *agape*: 1. LOVE FEAST. 2. Love.

I don't think the editors knew much more about *agape* than I, or if they did, they weren't spilling the beans. However, the ancient Greeks knew something about love. In addition to *agape*, they had terms that made two other important distinctions. *Philia* referred to friendship or fraternal love. *Eros* pointed to sex or eroticism. Perhaps I was thrown off by the common use of the expression "making love," which doesn't refer to opening the heart, but implies using another part of the body instead.

As I became more aware, I found that unconditional love is a central theme in all major religions of humankind. In the Christian Bible, Paul wrote a letter to adherents in Corinth that very clearly defined unconditional love:

> Love is very patient and kind, never jealous or envious, never boastful or proud, never haughty or selfish or rude. *Love does not demand its own way* (italics added). It is not irritable or touchy. It does not hold grudges and will hardly even notice when others do it wrong.

LOVE DOES NOT DEMAND ITS OWN WAY!!! How could it have taken me so long? I don't know. We awaken when we awaken!

What Schnapps Taught Me

It occurred to me that, other than my mother, I had few models of unconditional love in my life. As a child I had learned that I *should* love my mother and father because they did so much for me. And, of course, I was familiar with the term "romantic love," which often takes the form of an irrational, erotic compulsion that seizes you when one of cupid's arrows hits you in the behind. I was also aware that love among the father, mother, and children was supposed to hold a family together.

But for most of my life, I did not understand that unconditional love in my own heart is *essential for me* to live the most enjoyable life possible. I was not fully aware of what unconditional love was really about— even on an intellectual level.

A special clue did come to me one Christmas day when I was in my thirties. My mother walked in with a split loaf of French bread, a dachshund puppy inside it, and a jar of mustard on the side. I named the puppy Schnapps. Schnapps meant a great deal to me. She nestled at my feet all night long. Somehow she always knew when I planned to leave the house. She would wait by the front door and do her best to squeeze out to get to the car. I often took her with me. When I didn't, she'd yelp continuously, even after I had driven away. When I returned, she would run to me, jump up on me, wag her tail, and bark joyously as though my returning was the greatest thing that could happen in her life. Her love at that moment was unconditional.

I told myself that if I had been Schnapps, I would have sulked in the corner when my friend returned. I would have looked up and thought, "You wouldn't take me with you. I'm not going to let you know how glad I am that you're back, because you've hurt me." (Of course, Schnapps didn't have a rational mind capable of these concepts.) I told myself that I'd have it made in life if I could love as well as Schnapps!

Toddling Toward Love

While on retreat in Santa Cruz, I scanned the years of my life for the times I had felt love. My first memory of what I thought to be love was for Elizabeth in the sixth grade. Her desk was across the aisle from me, and beyond her was a window with bright sunshine outside. Under these conditions, her dress was usually slightly transparent and I could just see where her panties began. I never told her of my attraction, and my feeble attempts to talk to her almost never bore fruit.

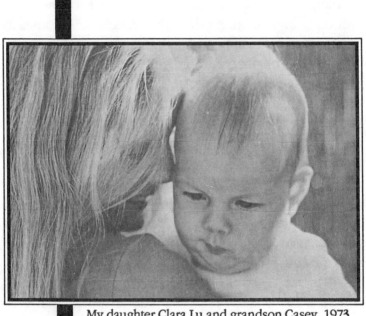

My daughter Clara Lu and grandson Casey, 1973

During my high school years, my affections grew for Beth. The Pancoast Hotel on Miami Beach had a dance every Saturday night, and Beth and I were on the invitation list. Since her house was on my way, I picked her up and brought her back home after the dance. After about two years of this, when graduation was imminent and I knew I would not be picking her up any more, I built up my courage. As she began to close her front door after saying good night, I blurted out through the rapidly narrowing opening, "I love you." She replied, "Thanks," and I seldom saw her again. My career of loving, whether *agape, eros,* or *philia* (it's hard to tell which), got off to a very slow start.

The first ongoing relationship in my life occurred with a Miami schoolteacher. It began during the period of my self-guided study after leaving Duke University. Florence was an intelligent, gentle, affectionate person. For the first time I created a relationship in which there was an openness on the physical level in terms of sex, on the emotional level in terms of caring, and on the intellectual level in terms of broad interests encompassing many areas.

This harmonious and rich relationship with Florence spanned about two years—but never evolved into marriage. My commitment was utterly lacking. I foolishly considered her too old for me. At that time in my life, my prejudice against age spoke louder to me than my actual experience of living.

Later Loves

Even through my marriages to Roberta and Bonita, I still hadn't learned about unconditional love. My programming had wanted them to be perfect—that is, to perfectly match the models in my head. I didn't realize that perfection in this way was impossible, that no one on earth would perfectly meet my models, and that I would never perfectly conform with anyone else's programming.

By the time I had gotten into Living Love, I knew a lot more about unconditional love. During many of the years at the Living Love Center, I was in a relationship with Lenore. She had beautiful childlike qualities and was deeply into Chögyam Trungpa's practice. I was comfortable with her being on a different spiritual path than Living Love, and I liked learning about it from her. But while she lived with me, she was critical of Living Love, which I felt interfered with the teaching that was going on there.

As founder of the Living Love system, I thought it was only helpful to point out Lenore's addictive demands to her. This was instantly met with resentment, resistance, and a lot of hurt feelings! It didn't take me too long to learn that I could effectively play teacher *or* lover—but combining the two roles with the same person does not work.

Live and learn. We loved being together, but there were some significant differences in our values. I was becoming clearer about what I wanted in a partner, and although I felt love for her, I knew that I did not want to be permanently involved with her.

Romi was another beautiful person in my life with whom I experienced deep feelings of love. I would have been open to a lasting relationship with her. We were on the motor home together moving from Cornucopia to California when she learned that her daughter was having problems, and Romi felt she needed to leave to be with her. I would have been willing to share her challenges with her, but that was not her choice.

Deeper Levels of Honesty

I remembered that when I lived on the *Caprice*, I thought I had to cleverly entice a woman to get her interested in me. I believed I had to be artful in setting up a woman's first sight of my paralyzed body with its withered limbs. Every now and then, when it was clear that we were going to bed together, I would go in my room and call my attendant to get me undressed, cover me up with a sheet, and turn on the music. With only a dim blue light, I would then call, "Yoo-hoo!" and she would open the door and come in. The possibility of heart-to-heart closeness in those days was limited by my mind-set. Fortunately I had come a long way since then.

Now I was viewing things differently. My new game was to be totally honest so a woman could perceive what she liked about me and what she didn't like. I stopped trying to maximize the former and minimize the latter. This made a relationship more realistic; it increased trust. Thus a woman would be more likely to turn herself off if I didn't fit her programming. And she would come toward me if I did appeal to her models. Either way, it would be better for both of us in the long run.

Another flip-flop! It was okay for a woman to see me unclothed with no elements of glamour. I liked that. It would turn off most women—and most likely they wouldn't have been potential partners for me anyway. It would save time for us both. But a woman who was not alienated by her programming when she saw the unadorned truth could be a good candidate for a relationship. With such honesty, there may be fewer dates—but I would increase the likelihood of solid communication, caring, and commitment. Why set myself up for a relationship that wouldn't work out?

Criteria for Marriage

In 1978 I was again without a partner and open to creating a lasting relationship. There were billions of people on earth. In my heart I could love everyone, but I couldn't possibly be involved with everyone. I was learning that love and involvement do not necessarily go together. Some people are so starved for love that they quickly jump in bed or into marriage if they sense any signs of genuine affection. Why marry in haste—and repent at leisure?

Developing my skill in loving unconditionally included distinguishing between love and involvement. What another person said and did could determine my involvement—but not my love. The key was to love *everyone* unconditionally. My involvement with someone in the soap opera of our daily lives would depend on whether I wanted to do things together. It was okay to throw someone out of my soap opera—but not to ever throw them out of my heart!

So I wanted to select wisely for enjoyment in marriage—instead of another great opportunity for growth! I arrived at a set of guidelines that would help me find what I was looking for.

First, I wanted us to mutually enjoy just *being* with each other. In the past I had found it easy to spend a lot of time with someone without ever experiencing whether I just liked being with her. We would go out to dinner, then to a show, then have a bite to eat, go home, etc. We would spend the evening *doing* things together—purposely chosen to furnish as much entertainment as possible. Now I was ready to simply enjoy a partner's presence.

The second thing I decided to look for was whether we really liked to do the same things together. Would I want to spend weekends reading and bird-watching while she really wanted to go hiking and play golf? We might create an otherwise satisfying relationship together, and yet the tugging and hauling over what to do might be more than we'd want. I wouldn't expect us to have 100 percent agreement, and yet it would be nice to enjoy playing most of life's games together.

And third, I wanted to be sure that we could be with each other's addictive programming. I realized that it would be unrealistic to expect no rough spots. The vital question was "How skillful can I be in dealing internally with my demands, and through it all, loving my partner unconditionally?" Without suppressing my true feelings, I didn't want to become emotionally defensive or judgmental if my partner's programming triggered lots of intense upset in her. And I concluded that a successful relationship would be more likely with a partner who also worked on her own separating programming.

It was at this time that I outlined these thoughts on how I planned to create my next relationship. Using the Living Love principles, I developed seven guidelines for preparing to go into a relationship and another seven for increasing harmony once I was in one. I put them into a book titled *A Conscious Person's Guide to Relationships.*

The Power of Love

I felt I was through with demanding a relationship. But I very much preferred having a helpmate who could assist me in writing and trainings, who was playful, and whose life had been enriched by the use of the Living Love methods. I was 57 and I wanted a woman who was physically and mentally strong enough to deal with the requirements of taking care of my body.

I determined that I would use the laboratory of my life to test the theory that unconditional heart-to-heart love is the key to creating the most satisfying life. I would test the hypothesis that if I could radiate my love unconditionally and continuously to my beloved, she would mirror this love back in sufficient quality and quantity to enable her to enjoy a great relationship with me *as I was*—even though I didn't fit all her models.

Could it be that at last I had a level of skill that could handle what is perhaps one of the most profound growth challenges a person can have—living happily with aliveness and intimacy with another human being? Was I ready to let my partner "be" and take responsibility for my upset feelings when they occurred? Would I be able to keep my heart open to continually love and serve my beloved? My inner voice said, "Yes, you are ready. You'll find more love and joy than you've ever known."

17

Finding Penny

It was time to practice what I preached in creating a life partnership. I had met Penny three years previously. Her father, Bill Hannig, had taken a weekend workshop I'd held in Phoenix. This workshop had made a big difference to him. One time when Penny was sick, he had loaned her all of my audio cassettes. She had found some answers she'd been looking for and was eager to learn more.

Penny was living in Rye, New York, where she worked as an aide at Rye Psychiatric Hospital and volunteered on the side as an Emergency Medical Technician. In the spring of 1976, I led a weekend workshop in Boston. Despite being on crutches with a broken foot, she borrowed a clutch-free car and made it to the workshop. This experience was so meaningful to her that she flew to Berkeley for the one-week workshop in July 1976 and returned again in March 1977 for a one-month training. She was also accepted onto the support team of the national tour that summer when we did workshops in Miami, New York City, and Chicago.

The motor home in which I had first made my way to California was now set up to carry a team of nine people plus sound equipment. Living for six weeks in an 8 x 35-foot vehicle gave us an opportunity to get to know each other. As we traveled east from Berkeley, each person was assigned rotating weekly jobs. They included cooking, housekeeping, and assisting me personally, which meant sleeping next to me at night and being awakened to turn me over about every hour or two. It also meant helping me with eating, toileting, bathing me in the little shower on the bus, and dressing me. Penny was one of those assigned to help me.

She was glad to get to know the founder of the Living Love system and to participate in supporting the weekend workshops. And she welcomed the opportunity to be close to me by assisting with my physical needs.

After several weeks on the motor home, I sensed that Penny was developing a romantic attachment to me. I appreciated Penny's loving attention and interest in me, but at that time I was already in a relationship with Romi, who was not on the trip. I discussed this with her and warned, "Don't get emotionally attached to being with me." I made it clear to her that I did not want to complicate my life by intimately relating to two people at the same time. It took a number of days for Penny to realize that she was indeed becoming attached. When she did, she did not take my advice.

When we returned to the Living Love Center in Berkeley, the bus team assisted in a week-long training. Penny began to inappropriately express her interest in me. In the middle of one training session, she walked up and kissed me—completely out of the blue. Another time when I was eating, Penny asked if she could stand next to me as I ate. Knowing this was coming from her increasing attachment to be with me, I said no. She did it anyway. After a few incidents like this, I called a meeting with Penny, Romi, Kris, and Carole. To assure Penny that I wasn't acting from separating feelings toward her, I told her several times that I appreciated her and had a love for her in my heart—and I did not want to be romantically involved with her. I was also concerned about the effect her behavior might have on the students. Penny left at the end of the workshop to travel to England as she had originally planned.

Exploring Our Relationship

In the summer of 1977 the staff and I had moved to Cornucopia. In the spring of 1978 when I left Cornucopia and returned to California, Romi had decided to live in Florida so she could be near her daughter. In October I phoned Cornucopia to talk with Carole. Penny was on duty at the front desk and answered the telephone. I was glad to learn that after traveling for a year, she had returned to complete her training for becoming a staff member. It was good hearing her voice again.

I remembered how much I had enjoyed Penny's company on the bus trip when she assisted me. Now that my life situation was different, I wondered if she might once again become interested in being with me. My heart felt warm at the thought. Without even the formality of dating, I decided to approach Penny directly and tell her what was on my mind. I was scheduled to fly to Cornucopia in November for Carole's wedding to Bill; this would give me a chance to talk with her.

The day after I arrived, I took a walk with Penny. Holding hands as we strolled around the grounds, I shared with her what I wanted. I told her that, if she was interested, I would like to explore our being together when she completed her apprenticeship at Cornucopia the following month. I recommended that we consider it for a few weeks before arriving at a decision.

I planned to return to Cornucopia at Christmas to give the Joy of Living training; she could give me her answer then. I suggested that if she felt good about our being together, she could fly to Santa Cruz and spend one month with me. I proposed that she then return to Cornucopia—no matter how things had gone. After being apart for one month, we would get in touch with each other and make a mutual decision on whether she would move out to Santa Cruz.

Why such an unusual arrangement? I figured that the desire for a relationship could easily sweep one or both of us over the falls of passion. I wanted the wisdom given by a balanced perspective of head and heart. If being together didn't seem like a good idea, making that decision with space between us would probably be easier. And if we were really supposed to be together, a whirlwind courtship would not be needed.

I experienced her as neither resistant nor eager. In her year of traveling, she had let go of her attachment to being with me. She had clearly not returned to Cornucopia in the hope of a relationship with me; she had simply come back because she wanted to be there for her own growth. She felt that living among people committed to personal growth was what she wanted in her life. She told me that when she had arrived at Cornucopia, she had assumed I'd be there. After three days she had found that I was living in California. This hadn't mattered to her since she was there for herself— not to be near me. We left our discussion at that, and after Carole's marriage ceremony I went back to California.

In late December on the night I was leaving for Kentucky, I was rolling too fast in my wheelchair and it tripped up on a piece of wood. I fell out and injured my neck and was not able to go to Cornucopia for the Christmas training. Once Penny learned we wouldn't be seeing each other, she wrote me a letter saying she thought she would like to try being together.

As soon as I got the letter, I phoned her and asked if she would come out to Santa Cruz in February to be with me for a month. She expressed apprehension about a sexual involvement as she had had little experience. I told her she would need to make that decision. She was also concerned that her parents might disapprove. I shared my thoughts that what was good for her would be good for them. She agreed, and said she would come to Santa Cruz. Less than two weeks later I met her at the San Jose airport with a pink carnation. On the drive home, she sat on my lap—the only empty seat left—in the front of the van. It felt wonderful being close to her.

The Ice Cream Parlor

Because I was becoming a well-known personal growth teacher, I was aware that some people tended to put me on a pedestal. They would assume I had every virtue that their programming requires a perfect teacher to have. Since I'm just a human being working on my own programming, this projection sets me up for quite a tumble in their opinion when they find I don't meet all their expectations. It's impossible for me to meet all of anyone's models—including my own. I want people to see me realistically.

With Penny, 1980

I sensed that Penny might have put me on a pedestal; she might even have developed an unquestioning openness to me. I didn't want her to regard my wisdom as more important than her own. I wanted to get beyond this phase with her as quickly as possible.

So the next day I took her to Old Uncle Gaylord's Ice Cream Parlor. Although she was heavily into candies, cookies, and other such goodies, I think she was trying to be on "good behavior." She ordered orange juice. I ordered a huge scoop of French vanilla ice cream on a crunchy sugar cone.

That incident helped clarify that fanaticism in the service of the good, the true, and the beautiful is not a part of the Living Love way. I try to be gentle with myself—and others. Since Gaylord's, we have avoided phony fronts on either side.

On Mission Drive in Santa Cruz, we lived in a pattern of voluntary simplicity. By 1979 I had donated almost everything I had to our nonprofit organization. I was living on a social security disability pension. (When my mother died in 1980, she left a $400,000 inheritance of which I donated about half and loaned the rest interest-free to the organization.) I have never received any salary or book royalties from our organization, although I do get room, board, medical care, the use of vehicles, and an annual vacation which I sometimes use and sometimes don't. This arrangement has felt comfortable to me, and to Penny as well.

In our first "home" together, our combination bedroom-office was about 9 x 12 feet, and my desk was 4 x 6 feet and used about one-fourth of the bedroom. Our clothes were stored in a small bookcase. We slept on the floor on a foam mattress that was folded up during the day. Although my wheelchair was able to go through the door to the desk, we had to take it out at night so we could close the door. If one's heart is filled with love, it's surprising how little one really needs to be happy!

During this month together, we were sexually intimate for the first time. We took many walks together and took pleasure in getting to know each other better. As we had planned, Penny left at the end of the month to go back to Cornucopia for us to assess from afar whether we wanted to share our lives together.

Near the end of the month apart, I already knew I wanted Penny to be my life partner. She fulfilled the guidelines I had formulated for a meaningful relationship. I enjoyed simply being with her whether we were doing anything or not. We had many common interests. I deeply valued that she was as committed as I was to using the Living Love methods for personal growth.

A staff member was leaving for St. Mary, and I asked him to deliver a message to Penny for me. On a piece of notepaper I inscribed three letters six inches high: "YES!" She, too, wanted to be with me. As they say in the skyrocket business, "It was a go."

18

Traveling Down the Road Together

Penny returned to Santa Cruz within a week and in April 1979 we began our life together. I had just completed the first draft of *How to Enjoy Your Life in Spite of It All*. When she came to be with me, we began editing it. I appreciated her knowledge of the Living Love system and her skill as a proofreader and clear thinker.

I especially liked the way we worked together in a largely egoless manner. Sometimes she would make a suggestion that I would reject. She had a keen way of sensing whether I really understood what she intended. When I didn't fully hear what she was recommending, she would keep insisting on her point over and over until I finally heard exactly what she was proposing. When she felt the communication was complete, she would then take the position, "Okay, you understand the suggestion. It's your book—you decide."

Her gentle and wise insistence frequently enabled me to go beyond my own particular way of explaining something so that it would be understood by more readers. It seemed that through our teamwork, we were able to turn out a better book than if I had done the job by myself. I felt so appreciative of the fun we had working together that I dedicated the book "To Penny—with whom I've experienced these truths more profoundly."

During the three years I was on retreat in Santa Cruz, Penny also helped me complete *A Conscious Person's Guide to Relationships* and assisted me with *Prescriptions for Happiness*. She and I began doing trainings together. I enjoyed working with her immensely. We gave two 30-day training programs at Harbin Hot Springs near Middletown, California, two weekend workshops in the San Jose Civic Center, and one at the Getting in Touch center outside Santa Cruz.

We lived in various locations around Santa Cruz with a few other people, hoping to eventually find a permanent West Coast training center. Each morning we all did exercises together, ate breakfast together, and used Living Love methods to work on whatever addictive programming had arisen.

The Monkey

One day a neighbor invited us to a video program at her home. There we met a fellow named Touchy the Clown (otherwise known as Dick Linebarger), who showed us *The Last Epidemic*, produced by Physicians for Social Responsibility. On the videotape, eminent scientists and military men warned of the possible destruction of the human race through nuclear weapons.

In the fall of 1980, within months after seeing this videotape, I was writing *The Hundredth Monkey*—a noncopyrighted book to help awaken humankind to the threat of nuclear annihilation. Penny assisted and supported me during this time.

The Hundredth Monkey did a good job of playing its part in waking us up. It was translated into nine languages, and we have printed and distributed over a million copies. A quarter million were given away.

Doing the Inner Work

From the beginning, Penny and I struck a chord of harmony and compatibility. We liked much of what we found in each other. On occasion, we both got opportunities to work on our separate-self programming. I had been using the Living Love system in my life ever since I had formulated it in 1972. Penny's determination to bring these methods effectively into her own life had begun in 1976. We were watchful for me-vs.-you demands and viewed them as destructive to what we really wanted most in our lives—to live a life of love through our unified-selves.

When Penny and I got together, she was somewhat overweight. During our first year in Santa Cruz, she slimmed down to 117 pounds. Her figure looked great to me. After achieving this fashion model slimness, she found she did not want to live with the calorie consciousness it required. So she let her weight return to around 135. As pounds went on, I discovered that my ego was attached to her maintaining a slim figure.

I noticed my clinging to the shape of things past, and I did not like my separate-self feeling of judgmentalness and disappointment. I especially did not want to trigger any guilt or self-rejection in Penny's programming about her body.

I decided to buckle down and use one of the common-sense methods I teach to others, called "Linking Separate-self Emotions With Your Demand."* So I pinpointed my demand: I was feeling disappointment because my programming was demanding that Penny not gain weight back. It was my demand—not Penny's pounds—that was making me feel disappointed and critical.

I knew my ego would let go of this demand that Penny remain slim if I focused on the trouble the demand was causing me. I realized my feelings of love had become slightly clouded. This negativity was starting to be picked up and mirrored back to me by her. As I became aware of the penalty I was paying by internally demanding that she stay slim, my mind began to let it go.

I imagined *preferring* that Penny stay slim instead of *demanding* it. I began to appreciate Penny as she was. That felt nicer. My mind cleared up and I could fully enjoy my sweetheart again.

Differences Don't Have to Make a Difference

Penny and I found that, like everyone else, we did not always agree with each other. We had no model that our opinions should always match; agreement is nice but not necessary. We saw ourselves as individuals with different programming, interests, aptitudes, and skills. Over the years we learned to accept our humanness and our diversity, and made it okay to play the soap opera of being two different individuals. It was an easy, gentle lesson for us. Recognizing that neither of us was perfect, we were confident that the love and methods we had

* Chapter 8 of *Gathering Power Through Insight and Love* fully explains this method.

would enable us to overcome any separating programmings over which our egos might clash.

While we were increasingly learning how firm to be with each other when we disagreed, we knew it was important not to harden our opposing positions into a battle line. We gradually worked toward the trust that love is more important than control, money, sex, pride, prestige, or anything else. The increasing harmony we felt in our hearts and our minds added much more to our happiness than having the ego satisfaction of being right or dominating or controlling the other person.

I found Penny to be very thorough and methodical. I tend to breeze through things to get them done so I can go on to what's next. I worked on fine-tuning my patience and appreciating even more deeply the balance we give to each other.

Trusting in Love

After many years of practice, most of my inner work was happening automatically in my mind. One of the few areas in which I consciously used Living Love methods was in Penny's refusal to share adult films with me. She did not like movies that showed frequent sexual activities. I occasionally enjoyed sensitive sexual movies that were being made for couples to enjoy together.

I was willing to let go of what my ego told me I could only get by using power. I affirmed to myself that I would not use me-vs.-her willpower to pressure her to give me what her programming could not give me with love in her heart. Power tends to kill heart-to-heart love.

I wanted to rely on loving, honest discussion to mutually work out new ways that enabled both of us to win. I totally trusted that the love in her heart would sooner or later give me what was gettable through love.

Penny and friend on a
conference trip to Australia

I was willing to let go of what wasn't gettable. Patience, openly communicating, and using the Living Love methods made it possible for us to find a win-win solution to this situation—and others that life threw at us.

Sometimes when I decided to let go of things I wanted that Penny didn't want, my separate-self ego said, "Suppose she takes advantage of your reluctance to use power?" And then my unified-self programming would step in and reply, "Her love gives me more than enough for me to be happy." And it has always worked that way for us.

Affordable Gifts

Early in our relationship, Penny told me that taking care of my physical needs 24 hours a day, seven days a week was too much for her. She felt she needed some time off. I didn't want Penny giving time, energy, or resources that she could not emotionally afford to give. It just wouldn't work. We decided that she would have one full "day off" every week.

After Penny's first day off, she forgot to take another one for over three weeks. She then realized that she no longer felt a need for such a break—and she felt good about having asked for what she had wanted at the time. As our years together went by, we found we could enjoy a partnership in which we were together almost 24 hours a day. We did not need space or distance from each other that may have been required earlier to recover from upsetting addictive demands. That pattern has continued, and it feels marvelous.

Each of us wants to give the other all we can afford to give without resenting it. And what we can give has seemed to increase as our heart-to-heart love has deepened. The programming I have today tells me that in general I experience the highest level of happiness and joy when Penny feels joyful and happy. Therefore, I've decided to put a top priority on loving and serving Penny. When I help Penny enjoy our life together, my own happiness takes care of itself.

This programming of supporting and helping my partner turned out to be particularly useful in the next few years. Although we were creating deeper levels of heart-to-heart feelings, Penny often had sharp and abrupt mood swings. The joy of living together would temporarily disappear—and then mysteriously return. We wondered what was happening.

19

Conquering Our Biggest Obstacle

My life with Penny flowed from one enjoyment to another—except every few days when she would switch from her usual light, loving frame of mind into a heavy, critical attitude. We tried to correlate the frequency of her depressions with her menstrual cycle, and anything else we could think of. But nothing seemed to be related.

Bonita's depressions had been lighter and had occurred with about the same random frequency. I had taken her depressions personally. I'd thought they meant she was not satisfied with our marriage. By the time I was with Penny, my ego no longer responded in a self-defensive way to such depressions. Bonita's depressions and jealousies had been the major factors that had led me to want to get out of the marriage. With Penny, I accepted them as an opportunity to love and serve her more deeply—to be there for her when she needed my help and understanding.

I remember saying to her, "We don't know what is causing these depressions, but together we're going to find out." We heard that sometimes zinc was helpful in improving one's moods. We tried it. It didn't work for Penny. We tried yeast. We tried one thing after another without results. We both knew that the mind affects the body. It is equally true that the body affects the mind. Penny blamed herself for her depressions, but since she had gained a high level of skill in using the Living Love methods in her daily life, I became quite sure that it was some malfunctioning of her body that was severely affecting her moods.

One day when we were in Garberville, California looking at places our organization might purchase for a training center, we talked with a woman who told us that her brother flew into a rage whenever he ate corn. When he stayed away from corn, he was consistently easy to get along with. She had learned that a person's particular biochemistry may respond to a food in a way that upsets the mind.

We eventually found a book entitled *Dr. Mandell's 5-Day Allergy Relief System* by Marshall Mandell, M.D. Penny read it and began following a food rotation system in which a given food is eaten no more than once every four days. But rotation alone didn't make enough difference for her. We needed to know more.

Back to Cornucopia

At Carole's request, we moved back to Kentucky in the fall of 1981 to work on setting up Vision Centers throughout the nation. These were to be local support groups that would broaden the outreach of our Living Love trainings.

Penny's mood swings were becoming stronger and more frequent. During some of those times she expressed doubt as to whether we should be together. I contented myself with the fact that we were together at that moment. I trusted that if it was fitting for us to stay together, we would.

That Christmas my father and his wife, Polly, sent us a three-layer box of assorted chocolates. Penny's attraction to candy led her to eat most of them within three days. For the following days she was negative, depressed, and tearful and hated herself, me, and everyone and everything around her. I had never known her to be so totally negative.

A cloud of gloom covered everything. I reminded myself that this was not her, just something that wasn't functioning right. I was hopeful that we would find an answer—and I was willing to accept this as a pattern in our lives if we didn't. I hesitated to say anything to her because just about everything brought a negative response—even loving and appreciative statements were rejected. For a few days she practically stopped talking to me. Nothing worked. At the end of three days, she began to pull out of it, and by the fourth day she was her usual bright, fun-loving self.

Although for two years we had been exploring whether Penny's depressions were due to food reactions, the dramatic cause/effect correlation between the unusually large amount of candy and her unusually severe mood became very evident to us. We had learned that it generally takes a little over three days for a food to be eliminated from the digestive tract. This was the time it had taken Penny to get back to her normal personality.

What could it be? Was it the sugar? Was it the chocolate? Or was it something else in the candy? Using the scientific food-testing procedures described in

Mandell's book, Penny eventually began, one at a time, to test many individual foods. She discovered that the corn syrup used in the candy was the culprit that had temporarily altered her biochemistry and changed the loving quality of her mind.

Food and Mood

At this point, Penny seriously delved into the new medical breakthrough called clinical ecology. She studied another book called *Brain Allergies: The Psychonutrient Connection* by William Philpott, M.D., an internationally known specialist. Through her reading she learned that most people are maladapted in some degree to one or more substances, such as certain foods, fumes from gas utilities in the home, and chlorine in the water. Their reactions are usually so blended and overlapped in daily life that they simply pass them off as "I have a headache," or "This is not my day," or "I must be getting old." Dr. Philpott explained that when proteins are incompletely digested, they form peptides, which create kinins that inflame tissues. If there is an inadequate function of the blood-brain barrier (a filter designed to keep undesirable substances from the brain cells), the mind may have mood swings or depressions.

Some forms of mental illness and even psychoses are known to be caused by maladaptive food reactions. In the foreword to Mandell's book, Dr. Abram Hoffer told of a 16-year-old schizophrenic on whom all previous treatments had proved futile. Out of the realization that she was doomed to a lifelong illness, he decided to see whether her schizophrenia was due to food responses. He put her on a water fast and within four days she was normal! Within an hour after drinking a glass of milk, her psychosis returned.

Penny, of course, never approached severe symptoms like this in her food responses. Although corn sugar and other forms of corn were a no-no, she found she was not reactive to cane sugar or raw honey. She avoided eating corn for the several years it took to strengthen her biochemical capacity. Guessing didn't work; every form of food had to be tested because the reactive patterns are different for each individual. Although there was much she still didn't know, we were beginning to understand what had brought on all those unwanted mood swings.

Moving to Coos Bay

In the spring of 1982 Carole left Cornucopia and joined another organization. Many of the staff went with her. Cornucopia was too much to take care of with its many acres and 100,000 square feet of buildings. I began consolidating our organization. I wanted a compact place that could be effectively operated by fewer people. I especially did not want the quality of the trainings to be drained by other activities like farming, building maintenance, and grounds upkeep.

Around this time, after the years of searching in California, Penny and I found a four-story hospital building in Coos Bay, Oregon that had not been used for years. The building was in need of major repair and remodeling. I was enthusiastic and could see it becoming a training center that would meet all our needs. Penny was less than enthralled at the sight of it but was willing to support me in my vision. It was available at a bargain price of $290,000. We were both drawn to the spectacular beauty of the Pacific coast. The air was clean, the climate mild, and trees and flowers grew abundantly. We closed Cornucopia, put it up for sale,

Ken Keyes College, Coos Bay, Oregon

and moved everything to the new Oregon location in September 1982.

The Paint Fumes

When we moved to Coos Bay, we began to paint the hallways and rooms in our new building. In the meantime, Penny had been painstakingly testing foods to discover which ones she was biochemically maladapted to. And then everything seemed to go backward—with a vengeance. She became more and more continuously depressed. Something had to be done. She felt she had tried everything she could on her own; now it was time for clinical help.

She looked into the Philpott Medical Center and decided to go. There she systematically retested one food after another. Her tests verified about two dozen foods to which she was maladapted in varying degrees. The list included wheat, corn, pasteurized dairy products, onion, garlic, apples, and oranges. Dr. Philpott not only tested foods; he also checked for chronic infections and for reactions to environmental substances. He found that Penny was reactive to chlorine in city water. He prescribed many vitamins and minerals to normalize her biochemistry so she might better handle airborne chemicals and safely bring reactive foods back into her diet.

After five weeks of testing, Penny returned to Oregon. She felt wonderful. Her body was cleared of the troublesome substances and chemicals. She knew how to avoid her problem foods. She was on a supplementation program that would build up her biochemical capacity, and she knew exactly how to retest foods in the future to see which ones could be brought back into her diet. The problem seemed solved!

Visiting Yosemite National Park
with Penny, 1980

We experienced the childlike glee of two people in love who hadn't seen each other for a long time. I could hardly wait to show her all the things we had done in remodeling our new center while she had been away. I took her to see the new guest rooms and the dining area, which had been enlarged and painted. Within minutes of seeing these rooms she became angry and depressed. And yet there had been nothing that had happened between us that could possibly explain her reaction.

After a few minutes' pondering, it became clear. Penny was reactive to latex paint! Since the building still had some painting going on, we arranged for her to avoid it for the next few weeks. It was not enough for the paint to dry; many of the chemicals in paint continue to come out for a period of weeks, although in decreasing amounts. Interestingly, Penny's only reaction to oil-based paint was to get a light headache, which went away when she left the area. Some people react to oil paint and are okay with latex paint. One's reaction is all on an individual basis.

Success at Last

With a deeper knowledge of her biochemical individuality, Penny began to live without the frequent depressions she had experienced since her college days. As she strengthened her biochemistry by taking nutritional supplements and avoiding substances to which she was maladapted, it became easier to pinpoint the cause of negative reactions. One day she and I were at a department store to find a Christmas gift for Clara Lu. At the perfume counter we had fun spraying samples on our wrists and necks. We made a selection and bought a bottle. On the way out of the store, Penny began to feel out of kilter. By the time we reached the parking lot, we could both tell that she was experiencing a reaction. She felt upset, insecure, and increasingly critical.

So we mentally checked back. What could it be? It was either demands, food, drink, or air. Was there anything that she was mentally demanding? No. Had she eaten anything that she wouldn't usually eat? No. Anything to drink? No. Had she breathed any air that might contain substances she could be reacting to? Yes. Our detective work had led us to the perfume.

At last our search for what to do about Penny's depressions had ended. We had met this challenge of life head-on—and together we had won. From the vantage point of this new knowledge, I think it's likely that Roberta's evening sleepiness and Bonita's depressions were biochemically related. Perhaps if I'd had the skill to be patient and accepting with them, the understanding and help would have come. I am thankful to now have methods that enable our relationship to flower under conditions that I had used to drag down my two previous marriages.

20

Enriching Our Lives Through Marriage

After Penny and I had been living together about a year, I told her I would like for us to get married. Penny felt she was not ready to be married at that time. That was okay with me; my programming did not create hurt, rejection, or any negativity. I wanted Penny to have all the time she wanted to complete whatever inner work she wished to do.

I told myself that every month we were growing closer and closer and creating a more joyful experience of life together. With this increasingly wonderful relationship in which we were both practicing Living Love, I felt that I could leave it up to Penny to decide when—or whether—we would be married.

Although she had greatly reduced her sensitivity to environmental substances, she was still vulnerable to PMS—premenstrual syndrome. These PMS effects were gradually diminishing with her continued use of minerals, vitamins, Chinese herbs, and other supplements she used with medical tests and supervision. As she had done since age 13, she was giving her body and mind the benefits of aerobic exercise. She understood the Living Love principles and was applying them in her life. Year by year her mood swings were decreasing.

Our Marriage at Shore Acres

As our time together went on, Penny did inner work on her yearning for us to have children, her desire to have a partner with whom she could go hiking, bicycling, and dancing, and her fear of my dying before her. The methods enabled her to effectively handle these issues. After we had been together for five years, Penny decided she was ready to be married. I was delighted.

Our parents had opposite ideas about our marriage. As an evangelical fundamentalist Presbyterian, my father felt that our living together broke the laws of God. He could not allow himself to feel close to us as long as we were "living in sin." He did, however, appreciate our occasional get-togethers for a meal when we visited him. So he was mightily in favor of marriage.

Penny's parents, on the other hand, felt good about our living together. Her father, Bill, recognized the benefits of the Living Love methods and had watched Penny becoming happier. When she was seriously considering marrying me, she asked him what he thought of it. Not wanting to push his opinion, he shared it reluctantly. He thought that she should not marry a man who was so much older than she.

He had good reasons for feeling that way. For many years, Bill and Ann, Penny's stepmother, had looked after two widowed mothers who each lived alone. One of them had been especially demanding of their time and attention. Perhaps without creating limits they could feel comfortable with, they felt burned-out with this over-dependence for so long. So naturally Bill didn't want to see his daughter stuck with an older person, whose needs would become greater and greater and who would most likely die long before her.

Penny deeply considered his comments. She wanted to use whatever wisdom her father was offering her—and she wanted to make the best possible decision for her own life. After sorting out her thoughts, she concluded that she wanted our marriage. Her father in no way tried to oppose the union, other than gently giving his input when Penny had asked him for it.

Both he and Ann were at our wedding with about 200 other guests on September 2, 1984 in the botanical garden of Shore Acres Park on the Pacific Ocean near Coos Bay. When we opened the ceremony for anyone to speak, he took the microphone and shared with the wedding guests:

> What a wonderful couple! Penny and Ken have encouraged and helped each other so much. We all know all the fine things that Ken has done and continues to do. For myself, I really respect and admire him, mainly because he is so genuine. He really *is* what he tries to help others to be. On behalf of Penny's family, Ken, welcome to the family.
>
> Over the last several years, as we've had some visits and a lot of phone calls from and to Penny, I've seen her grow in her happiness and contentment. She would be on a wonderful feeling of happiness. The next time we would be in touch with her a few weeks later, she had gone on to yet another more joyous level. It was just incredible. And it was consistent and steady, heartwarming, and beautiful to observe. I just wish you the very best, and I look forward to your traveling the glorious road that you're on

Giving Penny the wedding ring, 1984

I have always felt very close to Bill. I find it cosmically humorous that I am several years his senior. In many ways we are temperamentally and intellectually alike. Penny loves him very deeply, and perhaps this is part of why she likes to be with me.

Both Penny and I wrote our own marriage vows. During the ceremony we said the vows to each other that appear on the next page. We did not experience our marriage vows only as promises. They were also descriptions of the loving relationship we had already created during our years together. They just reaffirmed that the love in our hearts is more important than anything else.

We asked our many friends to send any wedding gifts in the form of a donation to the Union of Concerned Scientists, an organization working to reduce nuclear arms. Over $1,200 was raised for this worthy purpose.

The Joy of Marriage

I had told myself that getting married would not make any real difference to me—I felt as though we were married already in our hearts. And yet I was surprised that marriage did make a subtle difference. For both of us, it brought a deeper sense of commitment. Although there was no change in our day-to-day pattern, it seemed to give us a clear expression of our decision to be together for the rest of our lives.

It is said that happiness is being married to your best friend. This certainly applies to Penny and me. We like sharing a life of living love together. We feel that the added level of togetherness represented by our marriage ceremony has enhanced our love and devotion—and has helped us in our journey toward oneness.

Penny's Vows

Ken, I love you and I wish to marry you. With you, I find balance, clarity of purpose, acceptance, pleasure, mutually shared experiences and values, and growth through love greater than I have ever experienced with any one person. The longer I am with you, the more I love you and cherish what we have together. I want to share my life with you and to be close to you and your energy. These are my dreams, hopes, and wishes for my life with you: To share with you in offering loving service to our brothers and sisters. To learn from you of greatness. To work and play with you. To share your joys and sorrows. To celebrate and marvel with you at the wonder of life.

I vow to serve you and support you spiritually, emotionally, and physically. I vow to work on myself to take responsibility for all I experience, to avoid crystallizing separating thoughts and feelings toward you, and to keep love in my heart no matter what. I vow to continue to open myself to your love for me. I vow to build on my joys with you. I vow to stand by you and stay with you—in true happiness—as long as we both live.

Ken's Vows

The purpose of our marriage is to create a oneness in which both of us will be all we can be spiritually, mentally, and physically.

As my love for you grows within my heart, my energy increases for loving and serving you, my beloved, to help your life become richer and more beautiful. I experience a deep fulfillment and peace in just being in your presence. The state of marriage I choose to create today is an expression of my unconditional love for you, my deep appreciation of you, and my desire to spend the rest of my life with you.

Guided by the spirit of love, our energy will flow outward in loving and serving the world—so that the humanity that has nurtured us may develop a deeper and deeper unity and harmony.

Thank you for loving me, teaching me, showing me, holding me, caring for me, playing with me, choosing me.

Most of all, when my life ends on this planet, I want us to look into each other's eyes and be able to say, "Because we have loved each other, we have created a more wonderful adventure of life together."

What Lay Ahead

We kept ourselves busy with publications and trainings. We reorganized our training center to begin the Ken Keyes College, and we needed more trainers. Penny and I decided to conduct an intensive nine-month training course, beginning in September 1986, to certify Living Love trainers. We expected about 35 people to sign up for such a commitment. We were surprised when the enrollment reached 93!

With much help from the staff, we quickly remodeled the fourth floor, adding the needed extra dorm rooms. The students arrived and we got off to a grand start. It was exciting and stimulating to have such a large class. We spent long hours giving them all the attention and support we could.

Then, in the middle of the course on Christmas day, I picked up a flu-like virus that was going around. I seemed to throw it off in two days, but then I noticed a pain in my lungs. Penny took me to the emergency room of the local hospital. An X-ray showed that I had pneumonia. Little did I know that in the next few days my life would be hanging on a thread.

21

Winning the Pneumonia Game

I was given penicillin intravenously. At this point, my condition did not seem serious; the doctor wanted to keep me in the hospital simply to monitor me. Penny asked him if my condition could take a turn for the worse during the night. He said the chances of that happening were one in a thousand. But as the evening went on, my lungs continued to fill with fluid. Penny was given a chair that could be made into a bed so she could stay with me overnight. Although I was being given oxygen, the O_2 in my blood kept dropping.

That night Penny noticed that my breathing was getting very short—I could only say a few words per breath. I thought I saw someone holding a package and I asked what was in it. Penny said, "There's no one there." I began to marvel at the ingenious way the bathroom door and ceiling had bands of color that kept slowly swirling around. I was impressed that the hospital had provided this entertainment for its patients. I had no idea that I was hallucinating.

Penny saw my eyes start to roll up. She hurried to the nurses station to tell them what she was observing; the head nurse phoned the doctor at home. He had my arterial oxygen level checked—it had fallen dangerously low. Within minutes he was at the hospital and rushed me to intensive care. By this time I was semiconscious, so the doctor asked Penny for her permission to intubate me and explained the pros and cons: If I was not put on a respirator, my blood might not get enough oxygen; if I was put on a respirator, there was a chance that they might not be able to wean me off of it. The decision had to be made immediately. Penny consented. The doctor then turned to me and explained that he was going to put a respirator tube through my nose and throat into my lungs to provide oxygen. I would not be able to speak, whisper, or even swallow with the tube in.

The tube had to be forced between my vocal cords. Even though my body fought against the painful insertion, my mind felt relaxed and did not resist this soap opera. Once the insertion was over, I slipped into a vivid and pleasant dream-state for almost a day.

The Communication Challenge

The next few days were spent trying to communicate my physical needs for being turned every hour, being helped with a urinal, and frequently having my lungs suctioned of mucus since I couldn't cough it up myself. Between all these requirements, I saw this situation as an opportunity to take a welcomed rest from my full schedule at the college. Mostly, my consciousness was in the here-and-now moment.

Since I couldn't speak and wasn't strong enough to write, communicating with the nurses was difficult. Some were better at understanding what I wanted than others; they changed shifts every ten hours. It was a hit-and-miss process to get my simplest needs met. One time when I felt I needed to be suctioned, I tried to mouth the word "suction" to the nurse. She interpreted it as my asking for a kiss—which was definitely the farthest thing from my mind!

At that point I felt that Penny was the only person I could adequately communicate my needs to. Even though the staff was already generously letting her spend much more time with me than was officially allowed, I told myself I needed her help around the clock. How could I communicate this need? I was determined to give the doctor a full explanation of why I wanted Penny with me so there would be no reason for him to refuse. The message had to be spelled out letter by letter, word by word.

With me on my back and Penny holding an alphabet board so I could see it, she scanned the board with her finger and watched for a nod from me indicating each correct letter. This laborious process took a total of six hours. When complete, the whole message only took up one side of a small piece of paper. The doctor read the letter and promptly said, "No." In the long run that turned out to be a wise decision on his part; Penny was physically and emotionally exhausted trying to be with me in every way possible, and at the same time struggling with her addictive demand that I not die.

A Tight Spot

The hospital had a machine that clipped on my finger and constantly monitored the oxygen level in my blood.

Over three days, they tried to reduce the oxygen being given to me so the tube in my throat could be removed. Each time the respirator was reduced to a certain level, the reading of the oxygen in my blood fell too low. The longer a person is on a respirator, the harder it can be to get off it. My body was using all its strength with these efforts and getting weaker in the process. My muscles for breathing on my own were also weakening from lack of use. It didn't look good for me.

The tube I was hooked to rubbed and tore the inside of my nose raw every time I was moved. I could barely communicate. Yet in this situation, I noticed how calm and accepting I was through it all. I was once again grateful for my years of using the Living Love methods which, it turned out, had prepared me to cope with this ordeal. Although I was not far from death, I didn't think in such drastic terms. I did, however, recognize that I was in a tight spot.

Breath of Life

Through the years since my spiritual experience of oneness in the Exumas, an awareness of energy beyond my own ego had stayed with me in the background of my consciousness. That awareness was with me in my hospital bed. In my thoughts I silently said I would like to have additional time to love and serve on this earth. I was surrendered to whatever would happen, and yet I felt very willing to receive any help that would allow me to live so I could continue to serve.

On the first of January, I started to think, "One of these days they'll have to take this thing out, and I want to be ready to breathe again." I knew that my diaphragm muscles had been without exercise and that they needed strength for me to breathe on my own. I alternately

At my desk

In the garden

tensed and relaxed those muscles to build them up. Hour after hour I visualized increasing energy in them and also imagined that my lungs were very powerful.

There was a cuff on the end of the endotracheal tube that prevented the air from escaping back through my throat, thus forcing it down into my lungs. At 3 a.m. on January 2nd, the cuff collapsed and the tube had to be removed. The usual procedure is to replace it immediately to continue life support.

At the instant of removal, an intense energy filled my entire body. I began breathing strongly. My lungs became powerful—enough to immediately begin coughing up congested material. Being the only patient in the intensive care unit, I felt free to sing and shout for joy. Within one minute I had gone from having a respirator breathe for me to energetic, joyous living—breathing on my own. The nurses and doctor on duty could hardly believe it. After an hour, they had no choice but to agree that the recovery was real.

I spent another day in intensive care before going back up to the regular ward. The doctor had sternly instructed the staff to continuously monitor the oxygen level in my blood. It remained normal. What happened felt like a miracle. Sometimes it's easy to see special events like this as miraculous. To me all of life is a miracle.

In a World of Love

For the next two days I had incredible energy and my spirit soared. My world opened up again to include other people and their caring. I learned that everyone at the college had been sending me healing energy. Penny had been on the phone daily with my father, who had his congregation praying for me.

A beautiful trainer on our staff, named Aura, spent four hours with me. She brought a tape of a song that had just been written for me by Jai Michael Josefs. Two Christmas trainings had been under way at the college. Students from one class sent me purple chrysanthemums with a teddy bear. The students from the other class sent a little bonsai garden with bits and pieces from my own garden at home. Nestled among the tiny plants was a small ivory figure that they had each blessed on my behalf. It was accompanied by a card which they had all signed while I was still struggling for my life. The front of the card read, "Expect Miracles."

The day after I left the hospital, Penny and I spent the night camped at Bear Creek in the motor home, relishing the sounds of rushing water and the rustle of the forest leaves. My doctor had told Penny it would take me six months to fully recover. Within a week I was back to my normal life.

How thin is the thread of life we all hang on! Things can happen at any time that cause our lives to be cut short—accident, illness. Getting a mountaintop perspective of how we are all little dots in an infinite universe helps to cut my ego down to size—and humbles me.

The students from our nine-month trainer course graduated at the end of May. Right after that I got busy in what I felt might be my greatest contribution to humanity's future: how we can bring permanent peace and prosperity to our planet.

22

Loving and Serving in the World

Being able to return to my daily activities after pneumonia felt like a gift. I sensed the familiar internal richness of love that emerges from upleveling security, sensation, and power demands to preferences. I had more energy and enthusiasm than ever for contributing to humanity.

As I've moved closer to living consistently in my unified-self by letting go of my self-centered demands, I've enjoyed greater physical and mental relaxation, even though I may be busy and bustling in my everyday life. I've found an enormous increase in physical energy simply because of the growth of my unconditional love. And this helps me give even more of myself away by loving and serving others.

PlanetHood

While Penny and I were completing our work with the nine-month trainer students, my energy became

At the United Nations with Penny,
New York City, 1988

more and more directed toward getting out a book that would present a practical solution to the world's nuclear threat. We live today at a crucial time that can either extinguish all human life or open the door to realizing the wonderful potentials of our bodies, our minds, and our loving spirits. I regard humanity as now on the threshold of transforming itself into a new dimension of life on this planet.

Ever since writing *The Hundredth Monkey*, I had continued hunting for an answer that would really work to save humanity. In a course I led on world peace, one of the participants, Tom Hudgens, had given me a copy of his book, *Let's Abolish War*. In it he had explained a realistic way that would not require everyone on earth to love each other—for this won't happen in time. The ideas in Tom's book seemed excellent.

I started exploring the possibility of our organization publishing a popular book on this subject written by someone else who was more knowledgeable in the field than I. What evolved was an arrangement for me to coauthor a book with international lawyer Benjamin B. Ferencz. Ben had been a chief prosecutor at some of the Nuremburg War Crimes Trials, and had devoted much of his life to creating world peace through world law. Although we didn't meet face to face until after it was published in 1988, over the phone and through the mail we wrote *PlanetHood*—a nonprofit, noncopyrighted book.

The book explains eight steps you can take to insure that you and your children can have a future on earth. We ask people to rearrange their priorities in life and play their part in a *grassroots* movement of the people of this earth to save the world for themselves and their children. It tells how, by us all working together, we can replace the *law of force* with the *force of law*—to settle disputes *legally* instead of *lethally*. Many people, including the great Albert Einstein, have concluded that this is the only way to give humanity a long-term future.

While the book was in progress, I went to speak at a peace conference in Houston, Texas. In the back of the audience was Robert Muller, who had been the Assistant Secretary-General of the United Nations for 38 years, and was who now Chancellor of the World Peace University in Costa Rica. When my talk was over, he jumped up and passionately exclaimed that he agreed with everything I had said, and that this message must be widely spread. By the next morning he had written a press release for the videotape that had been made of my conference talk.

This unexpected response was the first of a chain of events that has left me amazed and hopeful. Students and staff at the college volunteered every weekend for months with contagious energy, packaging approximately 40,000 free copies of *PlanetHood* for mailing to peace groups, college professors, heads of state throughout the world, U.S. senators and representatives, and many other groups and individual decision-makers on the planet. Enthusiastic letters began coming in response to that massive mailing. Seventy thousand copies were also given free to the World Federalist Association, which actively sponsors the ideas in this vital book. Within the first six months of its release, 220,000 copies were printed. (We tapped the resources of the nonprofit organization I founded to pay for this costly effort. We figured money wouldn't be of much use if we let ourselves be wiped out by nuclear war.)

In the spring of 1988, Penny and I went to New York where we finally met Ben Ferencz. We found him to be

World Server Vow

Having taken the Living Love Vow to infuse the Living Love Way into the wellsprings of my thought and action, I now wish to unfold the energy of my life beyond my own self. Having experienced my own growth in the Living Love Way, I am now rich enough to give myself to the world—generously, openly, and without expectation of return. My goal is no longer my own enlightenment; it is to do my part in helping to relieve the suffering and alienation in the world. By taking the World Server Vow, I am dedicating my life to serving my brothers and sisters on this earth who are suffering from the pain of negative, separating emotions and confusion caused by addictive programming.

I vow to put the well-being of others above my own. No longer working toward self-aggrandizement, I will surrender my time, my comfort, my privacy, and my other ego-defended spaces to people. I will relate to the world appropriately and generously, and will skillfully put loving energy into the situations around me. Having developed compassion and love for myself, I can now offer it to others. I will work to reduce the addictive separateness in myself and in the world.

I will give up my striving for a separate, private life hunting for my own security, pleasure, and success. I will continuously offer myself to the world—even though I may be unrewarded, unappreciated, or rejected. As a world server, I will love and serve people selflessly as though everyone were my guest. I can be both gentle and energetic when interacting with people. By relating to life intelligently, openly, compassionately, patiently, fearlessly, nonaggressively, warmly, and delightfully, I will exercise greater responsibility to the world.

Transcending my own paranoia, vulnerability, and hesitation, I will respond wakefully to situations as they arise. Trusting myself, I will learn to correct my errors in perception or action in the moment when things are happening. Since my ego is no longer concerned with protecting my addictive demands, I can serve the world patiently and peacefully, and will not feel threatened by the world. I thus will become increasingly skillful and helpful in adding positive energy to our world.

I will use my life situations to perfect my use of the Twelve Pathways. At all times I will flow my energy into loving everyone unconditionally—including myself. I will thus become a lighthouse that can help people through the seas of illusion, separation, and hostility.

I will avoid foolish compassion, which is a shortsighted and cowardly attempt to gloss over situations—instead of responding wisely in a way that is truly nurturing to people. When the situation calls for it, I will be courageously direct (or even cutting) to appropriately relate to people instead of being timidly kind or politely agreeable.

By taking the World Server Vow, I am allying myself with the immense energy of all men and women who love and serve the world. I am forever joined with all who devote themselves to the growth of the spirit of love throughout the earth—and the liberation of sentient beings from addictive bondage.

by Ken Keyes, Jr.

a remarkable individual. The compatibility we had experienced throughout the phone calls and correspondence quickly developed into a warm and lasting bond of mutual appreciation and friendship. Ben and I spoke to delegates to the U.N. and nongovernmental organizations at a B'nai Brith luncheon across the street from the U.N. building. Then Penny and I went to Washington, D.C. where I had been invited to give a keynote address to the World Federalist Association. Once again, the reception by people who had long been actively working for world peace was touching and inspiring.

World Server Vow

Penny works almost full-time in publishing books and helping the Ken Keyes College. Like me, she has never accepted a salary for the books she's written or the work she's done, although her room and meals and basic living expenses are covered. We feel that it is a real privilege and pleasure to serve the world.

We have both taken the World Server Vow, which appears on the preceding page. We do not perfectly live by the vow; having taken it means that we have committed our lives to striving toward that ideal.

We are not self-sacrificing martyrs; we do it because it adds the highest happiness to our lives. Our life work has thus evolved into a blend of teaching inner peace to individuals and doing what we can to assist with outer peace among the nations of this earth.

23

Superlove With Penny

Penny and I create a great adventure of our lives together. We have twice been to Australia to speak at conferences. In our backyard we've created a bird sanctuary that sometimes attracts up to a hundred birds within 12 feet of our sliding glass door. She has learned to drive the 35-foot motor home, so we can occasionally get away for a few days by ourselves. When we were working on *Discovering the Secrets of Happiness*, we spent a month at an oceanfront apartment on Kauai. We enjoyed a four-wheel drive trip into the tropical jungle, sailboating at sunset, and flying in a helicopter to the bottom of Waialeale, the extinct volcano that made the island five million years ago.

We lead at least one training session in each workshop at the College when we are at home. Our lives have been enriched by personal contact with such wonderful people as Norman Cousins, Elisabeth Kübler-Ross, Wayne Dyer and his wife Marcie, and Jerry Jampolsky (Jerry is author of *Love Is Letting Go of Fear* and founder of Center for Attitudinal Healing) and Jerry's spiritual partner, Diane Cirincione. However, we mostly treasure the hours when we are alone together—just enjoying being with each other. We like snuggling in bed and watching videotapes Penny records from educational and movie channels.

Penny's love and interest in my family has enriched my relationships with my father and Polly, my step-mother, and with Clara Lu. We arrange time to be with Lu, Bob, and Casey whenever we are in Florida. Although he has occasionally visited us over the years, we've had relatively little close contact with my son Kenny.

Loving More—Demanding Less

The use of the Living Love methods has shown me how to surf on the waves of life instead of plowing under. As I live day by day with Penny, I either have a peaceful experience of just being here now with nothing special going on emotionally—or when something fits my preferential models, I create more fun and joy.

I have at last realized that the *real me* wants to love more and demand less—to open my heart to unconditional love no matter what my partner is doing or saying. I tell myself I can stay happy and loving no matter what happens. Living this philosophy more skillfully and effectively in my life continually smooths the path of genuine happiness for me.

It feels to me like Penny and I are beginning to go beyond the state of loving and into the state of oneness. I've come to realize that love still involves a subtle degree of separateness. For "I love you" to be descriptive, there must be an "I" who is separate from "you." There is still a subject (myself) and an object (my beloved). Even when the heart is expanding with feelings of love, there may still be overtones of separateness.

Going beyond "me" into oneness means that what's meant by "me" disappears and what's meant by "her" disappears in our conceptual experience. Instead there's just *us loving us*—playing the game of life as one hand washes the other. It's the ultimate in togetherness in which there is a mental and emotional merging of two to form one—and then back into the material plane as we interact in life together—one again becomes two.

Penny and I are thus experiencing an increasing amount of merging that has characteristics beyond the usual state we call "love." We still tell each other "I love you" because it feels so good to say these words frequently each day. What we call "oneness" includes all of the wonderful feelings of loving—and in addition it has an experiential unity and nonseparateness that might be described as "superlove."

We're Nothing Special

I don't want to imply that I'm in this expanded state all the time. But the old separate-self response patterns are becoming rarer. This is the wonderful bonus life is giving us as we both increase our skill with the methods we use.

As we experience what's happening in the relationships of other couples, our hearts reach out wishing we could offer more people the techniques that we've learned. Neither of us has the illusion that our great life together is due to anything unusual about either of us.

Boating with Penny near Coos Bay, 1987

Having fun with Penny in Kauai, 1988

We're just two people who have been fortunate enough to benefit from practicing some effective methods for loving more and demanding less.

Life Is My Teacher

Personal growth is a lifelong journey. There are a number of excellent methods (offered by us and other people-dedicated to teaching love) that can greatly enhance the voyage. And there are countless detours and dead ends that can hold us up for an entire lifetime—but only if we let them. I feel good today about how I have learned many of the lessons my melodramas have given me so that I could get on with my growth toward love and oneness. I feel deep appreciation toward the many people who have helped me play out my script on the cosmic stage of life.

I especially appreciate the role Penny has played in the latter part of my life. By the time we got together, I had worked through most of my heavy security, sensation, and power demands. Just as we can learn from pain, we also can learn from love, joy, and happiness. They confirm that we're on the right track. If a pilot crashes a plane, no doubt there are lessons to be learned. When the pilot lands successfully, a lesson is also learned. The programmings that achieved the successful flight are more deeply etched upon the mind, and skillful habits are thus more finely tuned.

Penny has helped me explore the experience that includes love and goes beyond toward oneness. With her wise feedback, I gently continue my growth without deep inner torment and striving. It just feels like drifting downstream to the ocean with an occasional turning to avoid the rocks. Today I can usually handle organizational "problems" without inside stress (I prefer to experience them as "challenges")—although they can keep me quite busy in the college and publishing dramas of my daily life.

I've experienced that love seems to create a nurturing shield that insures that I'll always have enough to be happy. It protects me from danger. It helps me get away from the pain of separateness—and helps me stay aware of the harmony and happiness I can create with the people around me.

The World Is My Mirror

Living Love shows me how I can create a harmonious world for myself that adds to the quality of my life and can contribute to those who follow after me. It helps me develop compassion and heart-to-heart caring.

My life has taught me that the world is my mirror. If I give out separateness, usually people respond with separateness. If I give out loving and caring, I generally get back loving and caring. Sometimes I tell myself that I don't like a person I have met. Instead of criticizing him or her in my mind, I try to look within myself to see if his or her behavior is simply reminding me about parts of myself that I don't like. I try not to blame myself, but search for where I can transform my attitudes and thus feel more understanding, compassion, and appreciation for everyone. When I don't like what's happening, I find it's more helpful to remember the mirror—and let go of the magnifying glass.

I believe each of us has a divine essence with the godlike ability to create our experience of the world.

Everyone is a powerful creator of separateness or love and unity in his or her own moment-to-moment journey through life.   Appreciating and loving ourselves and others is the goal of personal growth.   To the extent that we can understand with our heads and love with our hearts, we will know true happiness.

Remembering this, I can thus empower myself to go from playing "victim" to consciously becoming a "creative cause."   And by increasingly harnessing the power of unconditional love in my life, I am able to say at last, "THIS IS IT!"

Appendixes

Appendix 1
The Secrets of Happiness

When people ask me why I got into Living Love, I reply, "I guess it was because I needed it so much." The purpose of personal growth is to be happy *here and now*—not *if and when* things change in exactly the way my present desires dictate. The mind is always capable of wanting something it does not have—demands are infinite. But it's possible to rearrange our programming so we can enjoy life as it is—instead of longing for life as it isn't.

I want to give an overview of some of the "secrets" that opened the way to my rapid personal growth toward loving more and demanding less. To understand these valuable "secrets," please become familiar with the Living Love terms on the next page.

Outside and Inside

We all know that life is really lived on the inside—in one's feelings or emotions. And what is it that generates our emotions? Our answer to this is crucial—and 99 percent of the time we get it wrong! We usually tend to think our emotions are primarily caused by what happens outside—what is said and done around us. We hear such erroneous thinking in statements like "You make me angry." But the *immediate* cause of our experience is inside us—not outside. It's our *inside*

Living Love Terms

Here are six terms that help me share with you the details of my inside personal growth:

DEMAND or ADDICTIVE DEMAND: A programming or operating instruction in the mind that makes me upset or unhappy if it is not satisfied. A desire that I think I must have to feel happy. Wants and desires are demands if they trigger such emotions as fear, frustration, or anger when I don't have what I want. For example, "My programming demands that I not get caught in a traffic jam."

PREFERENCE: A want or desire that does not trigger separating emotions or tensions in my body or mind whether or not it is satisfied. Using preferential programming, I can try to make changes, I can think I am right, but I emotionally accept what's happening. For example, "I prefer not to get caught in traffic, but I'm not making myself upset if I do."

PROGRAMMING: Learning, habits of mind, behavior patterns. Conscious or unconscious instructions installed in my mind that determine my feelings and guide my thoughts and actions. For example, "My programming is making me angry when I get caught in traffic," or "I have programming that says I can feel patient in a traffic jam."

SEPARATE-SELF: The illusory "me-vs.-them" perceptions that guard my security, sensation, and power demands. The mental programs that create the experience of life as a battle against myself, other people, and the world. For example, "My separate-self is mad about getting caught in the traffic jam, and I feel angry toward the other drivers."

UNIFIED-SELF: "Me-and-them" instead of "me-vs.-them" programming. Programming that gives me an overall perspective of how everything fits into my journey through life, either for my *growth* or for my *enjoyment.* My unified-self thus creates an experience of people and situations as a unified or integral part of my journey instead of a nuisance or threat. For example, "My unified-self patiently accepts the traffic jam."

UPLEVEL: To change a demand into a preference. For example, "I upleveled my demand that I not get caught in traffic, although I still have a preference that I avoid traffic congestion."

programming that really makes us angry—not the other person or even what the other person did.

Our feelings don't necessarily tell us how we should assess a situation. They *do* indicate whether our desire about that situation is demanding or preferential.

Here's the way it works: Our minds automatically compare moment by moment what is happening now with our models, expectations, and desires. If we have a demanding program and we're not getting what we're demanding, we trigger feelings of fear, frustration, anger, or other separateness—which add up to unhappiness.

We've all accumulated many demanding programs in our minds. Life being what it is, we usually don't stay peaceful, loving, and happy for long. We usually fluctuate throughout the day between making ourselves upset or enjoying our lives.

One person may appreciate your suggestions about how to wash the car; another may feel upset or angry and think that your suggestions imply that s/he isn't smart enough to wash a car without your help. Thus, a person's emotional response has nothing to do with the suggestions you offer. It is fundamentally generated by the programming in their mind—their values, attitudes, memories, etc. It is crucial to understand that your suggestion does not create appreciation or resentment in another person—it is their *programming* that basically determines their reactions.

The Ego's Deception

Our programming constantly misleads us. It fools us into looking outside—when both the problem and the solution are inside. It makes us look at other people or events that trigger our internal experience, and blame them for it—instead of pointing our fingers at the real culprit—our *negative, separating programming.*

One time my girlfriend was late for dinner and I felt irritated. What was the immediate, practical cause of my irritation? My partner's lateness? Or was it my own programming that triggered my feelings of irritation?

My *separate-self* blamed my partner when I felt irritated! But my *separate-self* was actually wrong when it said, "You make me angry when you're late." My mind sees things not as they are—but as I am programmed to see them. The truth of the matter was that my own demanding *programming* made me irritated. This diagram shows that my partner's lateness was an *outside event*—a part of the soap opera of my life:

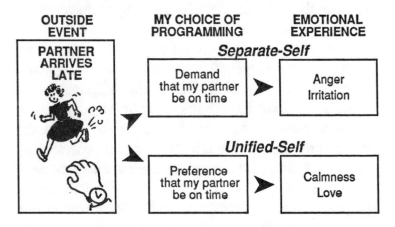

OUTSIDE EVENT	MY CHOICE OF PROGRAMMING	EMOTIONAL EXPERIENCE
PARTNER ARRIVES LATE	*Separate-Self*	
	Demand that my partner be on time	Anger Irritation
	Unified-Self	
	Preference that my partner be on time	Calmness Love

If I change my programming so that I *prefer* that my partner be on time instead of *demanding* it, I would not feel upset. I would not hook myself into feeling anger toward my partner. I could feel calmness and love. I've learned to blame *my own programming* (instead of my partner or anyone else) for any unpleasant or separating emotions I create in myself. Please notice, I don't blame *myself* for feeling irritated. *I blame my demanding programming*.

There may be some consequences to my girlfriend's being late. Perhaps there's a lesson to be learned by me or her. I can even ask that she try to avoid being late in the future. However, I do not have to make myself feel irritated when she doesn't arrive promptly. And whenever she does show up, we'll both have a lot more fun if I'm not upset over the timing.

Addictive demands give us a double disadvantage. It may upset our evening plans if she's late. Why add the additional disadvantage of one or both of us being upset? No matter what happens, I'm better off with preferential programming.

If I choose to use them, the Living Love methods usually make it a lot easier for me to change my own programming than to change my partner—or get her to admit she's wrong. My life is enriched by having this option. I've found that changing my own programming is possible. Changing someone else's programming may be impossible! This doesn't mean that I can't *lovingly* try to help my partner be on time. The key is "lovingly."

The Way to Happiness

Both demands and preferences create happy feelings when I get what I want. The enormous difference between these two programmings occurs when I don't get what I want—which happens frequently in my life— and I bet in yours, too.

Here is how my preferences add to my happiness— whereas my demands set me up for unhappiness. Sometimes I get what I want—and sometimes I don't.

We Can Choose

Here are some of the emotions triggered when things don't go the way we want them to. (Some emotions, such as jealousy, may be activated in any of the first three categories.)

Security Emotions

Fear, apprehension, worry, dread, nervousness, despondency, bitterness, dismay, mournfulness, anxiety, panic, terror, horror, despair, regret, hopelessness, insecurity, disappointment, hurt, sadness, helplessness, grief, loneliness, powerlessness, shame, alienation, guilt, confusion, embarrassment, envy, doubt, jealousy, dejection, alarm, isolation, discouragement.

Sensation Emotions

Frustration, boredom, discouragement, disappointment, jealousy, grief, dismay, alienation, disgust, envy.

Power Emotions

Anger, annoyance, irritation, impatience, frustration, aggravation, exasperation, resentment, alienation, indignation, hostility, disdain, revulsion, hate, rage, fury, wrath, powerlessness, jealousy, malice.

Loving Emotions

As we go beyond the destructive, demanding habits of mind, the *same life situations* may now trigger these enjoyable feelings:

Love, acceptance, contentment, peace, tranquility, enthusiasm, calmness, friendliness, delight, satisfaction, affection, happiness, togetherness, gladness, humility, tenderness, harmony, merriment, compassion, appreciation, lightheartedness, relaxation, cheerfulness, buoyancy, closeness, warmheartedness, joviality, benevolence, intimacy, serenity, enjoyment, understanding, courage, safety, empathy, inspiration.

Reproduced from
Gathering Power Through Insight and Love
by Ken and Penny Keyes.

With a demanding program, I feel great only when life meets my model. When it doesn't, I trigger such emotions as fear, frustration, anger, resentment, grief, irritation, or hurt. These add up to unhappiness (or even suffering) when prolonged. With many demanding programs, my life often ran one overlapping set of negative, separating emotions after another. Unhappiness became chronic. (For insight into our emotions, please read "We Can Choose" on the preceding page.)

The Happiness Game

The happiness game requires me to uplevel my demands to preferences. Let's look again at this process:

Demands set me up for experiences varying from complete disaster to briefly wonderful—depending on whether I get what I want. But even if my demand gets met, I'll probably want more or better—or I'll worry about losing what I've got. Demanding is ultimately self-defeating. As long as I have demands, my happiness is not under my control.

As a preference, a desire will make me feel good when I get what I want. And when I don't get my preference, *I still feel okay.* That's the neat thing about preferences. Preferences set me up for feelings ranging from calm to wonderful. I win no matter what life gives me!

Demanding programs that can destroy the enjoyment of my life are like barnacles on the bottom of a boat. They are not a part of the boat; they cling to the bottom and destroy the performance of the boat. An intelligent sailor doesn't criticize the boat; s/he just scrapes the barnacles off the bottom.

With Penny in a training room
at Ken Keyes College

Acquiring higher and higher levels of skill in using these secrets of happiness in one's moment-to-moment living is a lifetime challenge. The rewards are a happier and more fulfilling life. To me, that's what personal growth is all about.

A class session at Ken Keyes College

Appendix 2
The Ken Keyes College

I founded the college as a nonprofit educational organization to offer Science of Happiness trainings at low-cost prices. While the principles of Living Love are well explained in the books listed in Appendix 3, about 25,000 people of diverse religions and nationalities have found our gentle workshops especially helpful. They particularly appreciate the loving environment, personal guidance, and hands-on experience in applying our practical techniques in their own lives.

These trainings are designed to be both entertaining and challenging. Personal breakthroughs from some of the internal roadblocks that cause us fear, frustration, and anger are to be expected in these trainings. The emphasis in all of the trainings is to learn how to use practical methods to open your heart to appreciate and love yourself—and other people. Countless marriages have been saved and individual lives lightened through the lasting improvement offered by these life-enriching workshops.

Some of our trainings are: Joy of Living, Healing Your Inner Child, Increasing Your Self-Esteem, Adult Children of Alcoholics, Self-Appreciation, Gathering Power Through Insight and Love, and Finding Inner Peace. We give workshops in other cities in the United States and Canada. You can call the Registrar for information on trainings near you. At the college the cost is around $395 for a one-week training or up to $1895 for a ten-week training, which includes a comfortable dormitory room, food, and instruction. Our prices are low because most of our staff of talented and experienced men and women voluntarily serve at base wages (plus bonuses if there is a surplus).

I invite you to experience our loving workshops, which are held in an environment offering natural beauty and recreational opportunities. Across the street from the college are public tennis courts, a heated swimming pool, a softball diamond, jogging trails, and a delightful duck pond. Nearby are some of the most beautiful beaches and forests in the country. Located on scenic U.S. 101 on the Oregon coast, Coos Bay is easily accessible by car, bus, or air. Give yourself a gift you will cherish for a lifetime and come visit us soon.

For a free catalog, you can write to the Registrar, Ken Keyes College, 790 Commercial Avenue, Coos Bay, Oregon 97420, or telephone (503) 267-6412. Once on our mailing list, you will receive information about new books, audio and video cassettes, posters, and workshops.

Appendix 3
Other Books by Ken

Here are books that explain the methods which Penny and I needed to create inner peace in our own lives. The techniques presented have enriched the great adventure of life we share today. To date there are over three million copies of these books in print. We invite you to enjoy and benefit from them. We hope they may be equally helpful to you.

Handbook to Higher Consciousness
Ken Keyes, Jr., $6.95

Why are our lives filled with turmoil and worry? Why do we allow ourselves only small dribbles of peace, love, and happiness? *Handbook to Higher Consciousness* presents practical methods that can help you create happiness and unconditional love in your life. Countless people have experienced a dramatic change in their lives from the time they began applying the effective techniques explained in the *Handbook*. There are over one million in print worldwide.

Gathering Power Through Insight and Love
Ken and Penny Keyes, $6.95

Here's how to do it! This outstanding book gives you detailed instructions on exactly how to develop the love inside you. It describes the 2-4-4 system for going from the separate-self to the unified-self: 2 Wisdom Principles, 4 Living Love Methods, and 4 Dynamic Processes. This book is based on our years of leading workshops. These skills are essential for those who want the most rapid rate of personal growth using the Science of Happiness.

A Conscious Person's Guide to Relationships
Ken Keyes, Jr., $5.95

If you're looking for effective new ways to give yourself a love-filled, satisfying, wonderful relationship, you will discover them in this book. Here finally is love without tears! This book contains seven guidelines for entering into a relationship, seven for being in one, and seven for decreasing your involvement with gentleness. It describes sound principles that many people have found invaluable in creating a loving relationship. Over 250,000 in print.

How to Enjoy Your Life in Spite of It All
Ken Keyes, Jr., $5.50

Learn to enjoy your life no matter what others say or do! The Twelve Pathways explained in this book are a modern, practical condensation of thousands of years of accumulated wisdom. Using these proven pathways will help you change your thoughts from separating, automatic reactions to practical, loving ways of thinking. They promote deep levels of insight, and help bring increased energy, inner peace, love, and perceptiveness into your moment-to-moment living. A must for people who are sincerely interested in their personal growth. 80,000 in print.

Your Life Is a Gift
Ken Keyes, Jr., $5.95

Written in a lighthearted yet insightful fashion, here is a wonderful introduction to ways you can create your own happiness. This charming book, geared toward those embarking on personal growth, shows how simple it is to experience life with joy and purpose by insightfully guiding your thoughts and actions. Filled with amusing and endearing drawings, this is a treasured gift book for all ages. 175,000 in print.

Prescriptions for Happiness
Ken Keyes, Jr., $4.95

Use these easy-to-remember secrets for happiness. Works for both
children and adults. Designed for
busy people, this book can be
absorbed in about an hour. These
simple prescriptions work wonders.
They help you put more fun and
aliveness into your interactions with people. Learn to
ask for what you want with love in your heart. Benefit
from techniques that boost insight, love, and enjoyment
in our uncertain world. Some people, after reading this
book, buy out the bookstore and give copies to their
friends. 144,000 in print.

Taming Your Mind
Ken Keyes, Jr., $6.95

This enjoyable classic (which has
been in print for 35 years and is more
relevant today than ever) shows you
how to transform your rational mind
into a useful servant. These important "Tools for Thinking" can
enormously improve your success in
making sound decisions, getting along with people,
being more effective in business—and working with
others to build a better world. Written in an entertaining
style with drawings by cartoonist Ted Key, it was adopted
by two national book clubs. Over 100,000 copies in
print.

Your Heart's Desire— A Loving Relationship
Ken Keyes, Jr., $4.95

Do you want to bring the magic of enduring love into your relationship? All of us have had a taste of what heart-to-heart love is like. We cherish those times and strive to experience them continuously. Using your rich inner resources, this book can inspire you to create a more loving relationship—without your partner having to change! It can help you to beautifully deepen the harmony, love, empathy, and trust in your relationship.

The Hundredth Monkey
Ken Keyes, Jr., Pocketbook, $2.00

There is no cure for nuclear war— ONLY PREVENTION! This book shows you that we have the creativity and power to change both ourselves and the world. You are introduced to a radical new way of realizing the impact of your energy on the world around you—a quantum leap in consciousness. You'll find here the facts about our nuclear predicament that some people don't want you to know. May be read in a little over an hour. Internationally acclaimed; over one million copies have been distributed throughout the world. This dynamic little book has been translated into nine languages, including Russian.

PlanetHood
Benjamin B. Ferencz and Ken Keyes, Jr., Pocketbook, $2.50

This breakthrough book, which is the sequel to *The Hundredth Monkey*, explains how you can personally give yourself and your family a future in this nuclear age. It tells how we can replace the *law of force* with the *force of law*. It explains eight ways you can personally help the world settle disputes *legally*—instead of *lethally*! Discover this workable, practical way you can create prosperity and permanent peace on our planet. 220,000 in print. Released March 1988.

Meeting the Challenge

You can empower yourself to make a difference. Since your future and the life of your family may depend on rapidly replacing the law of force with the force of law, we are making *PlanetHood* available on a nonprofit basis. Please buy as many copies as you can and distribute them quickly. To help you do this, the list price of *PlanetHood* is $2.50. For only $3 postpaid, we will mail a copy of this book to any person in the world for whom you furnish the name and address. If you buy a case of 100, we will mail the case anywhere in the United States at a cost of only 70¢ per book (a total of $70 postpaid in the U.S.). If you buy 1,000 or more, they will cost only 50¢ per book (a total of $500 including shipping in the U.S.). Send orders to Ken Keyes College Bookroom, 790 Commercial Avenue, Coos Bay, OR 97420. For VISA or MasterCard call (503) 267-4112.

All these books are available in bookstores
or see page 231 for order form.

Two powerful workshops on tape!

TO ORDER BOOKS AND TAPES

Qty.	Item	Price	Amount
	Handbook to Higher Consciousness	$6.95	
	Handbook to Higher Consciousness Workbook Available Spring 1989	$3.95	
	Handbook to Higher Consciousness (Cassette)	$9.95	
	Discovering the Secrets of Happiness: My Intimate Story	$7.95	
	A Conscious Person's Guide to Relationships	$5.95	
	Gathering Power Through Insight and Love	$6.95	
	Gathering Power Through Insight and Love (Cassettes)	$15.95	
	How to Enjoy Your Life in Spite of It All	$5.50	
	Your Life Is a Gift—So Make the Most of It!	$5.95	
	Prescriptions for Happiness	$4.95	
	Taming Your Mind	$6.95	
	Your Heart's Desire—A Loving Relationship	$4.95	
	The Hundredth Monkey	$2.00	
	PlanetHood—The Key to Your Survival and Prosperity	$2.50	

Please include shipping and handling charges: $1.50 for the first item, 50¢ for each additional item. **SPECIAL OFFER: If you order 10 items or more you can take off 20%, PLUS we'll pay for shipping and handling.**

Subtotal	
Shipping	
TOTAL	

☐ **Yes!** Please put me on your free mailing list and send me a free catalog listing workshops, books, posters, music albums and cassettes, and audio and video tapes.

Ship to: (please print) _____

Address _____

City _____

State _____ ZIP _____

Telephone No. ( ) _____

For VISA or MasterCard orders only:
Card # _____

Exp. date _____ Signature: _____

Send order along with your check or money order to: Ken Keyes College Bookroom, Dept. DSOH, 790 Commercial Avenue, Coos Bay, OR 97420. To order by phone with VISA or MasterCard call: (503) 267-4112. Call Monday through Friday 9 a.m. to 4 p.m. (PST). Allow up to 4 weeks for delivery via fourth class mail.